The Holy Latin Vulgate Bible 1592
&
1 John 5:7 (Comma Johanneum)

Is the Douai (1582) & Reims (1609) a Faithful Translation of The Holy Latin Vulgate (1592 edition) Bible?

by

William J. DeTucci

The Holy Latin Vulgate Bible 1592

&

1 John 5:7 (Comma Johanneum)

ISBN: 978-1-300-87469-0

Dedicated to Saint Jerome & Pope Clement VIII

Table of Contents

Saint Jerome Biography

Jerome (Latin: *Eusebius Sophronius Hieronymus*; Greek: *Εὐσέβιος Σωφρόνιος Ἱερώνυμος*; (330 – 30th September 420 † A.D.); his feast day is celebrated on September 30th, his birth place was in (Stridon, in Dalmatia, a Roman Province)[1], in addition, he is one of twenty-nine (29) Doctors of the Church, he was a priest, confessor, theologian, translator, and historian; Pope Benedict XV (21st November 1854 – 22nd January 1922 A.D.) called Saint Jerome "The Great Doctor"[2] *in explaining the Sacred-Scriptures* (The Bible). In his quest he not only illuminated the understanding of Scripture but even expounded upon it in a way that is overwhelming God-like. At the time of his birth until around his teens and little after did Saint Jerome struggle with lust (fornication) that nasty vice that is the pith of the overwhelming majority of men and women into Satan's trap and disguise to lure (bait) us from God the font of Purity, Wisdom, and Hope. Saint Jerome lamented (mourned) his past by these words:

---

[1] **Saint Prosper of Aquitaine** (a lay theologian) "attests" to this for his life overlapped that of Jerome: ***Epitoma chronicon*** (MGH *auct. ant. ix*, 451 and 469). P. Hamblenne (art. cit. below, 1113) seeks to eliminate the inconsistency by arguing, on the basis of the reading of V, the most ancient of the MSS, that Prosper in fact dated Jerome's birth in 330 A.D.; Cf. **Jerome**: *His Life, Writings, and Controversies*, by J.N.D. Kelly (John Norman Davidson), Published by Gerald Duckworth & Co., Great Britain, 1975, p. 337.

[2] Papal Encyclical ***SPIRITUS PARACLITUS*** (September 15th 1920) Article # 1.

"How often, when I was living in the desert, in the vast solitude which gives to hermits a savage dwelling-place, parched by a burning sun, how often did I fancy myself among the pleasures of Rome! I used to sit alone because I was filled with bitterness."[3]

However, God (Christ) gives us so many opportunities and graces to see and defend ourselves from that nasty serpent the Devil (Satan)[4]. Don't give up! And, do not give into to temptation and despair. No one can enter Heaven without the aid of God (Christ) and His Holiness[5], (the Sacrament of Baptism)[6] and the True Catholic Faith[7]; just as man

---

[3] Saint Jerome ***to Eustochium*** (dated 376/7), Letter 22, 7.

[4] Isaias 14:12; *Lucifer=Light Bearer*! The Greatest Saint of the Most Holy Catholic Church is the Holy Mother of God, Mary Ever-Virgin! She (Mary) would be hailed (Luke 1:28) and be brought to The Light (Genesis 3:15) and She would separate (Apocalypse 12:17) Her Seed (Offspring) to that of the Seed (Offspring) of Lucifer, the Devil—the father of all lies, lust, heresies, and evil (John 8:44).

[5] Pope Boniface VIII "defined" which was always true that: in ***Unam Sanctam*** (November 18th 1302 A.D.) that it is *absolutely necessary* to be Subject to the Roman Pontiff; what would happen if the Roman Pontiff defected from the Papacy or died, etc…we must hold to the Teaching of the Pope at the time that he was installed as Head of the (Christ's) Catholic Church upon earth.

[6] John 3:5.

[7] The Vatican Council (1869-1870 A.D.) under His Holiness of Blessed Memory Pope Pius IX (13th May 1792 – 7th February 1878), Session 2, Janurary 6th 1870 A.D; Cf. ***Decrees of the Ecumenical Councils***, Volume Two: Trent to Vatican II, Edited by Norman P. Tanner, S.J., Published by Sheed & Ward, Georgetown University, 1990, p. 803.

cannot save himself[8] from eternal ruin; man therefore is *absolutely* in need of a Saviour, Our Lord and Saviour[9] Jesus Christ (True God and True Man = One Person)[10]. Who is it that conquered All-lust and All-heresy but He that arose[11] (risen) from the Dead (of His own Power)[12] and sits now at the Father's right hand[13] of whom Christ (God) will come to judge[14] the world? Saint Jerome in addition, translated from the Hebrew[15], Aramaic, Greek, and Latin in the Old & New Testaments.

[8] Romans 3:23; this however does not apply Christ (God) and to the Blessed Virgin Mary (The Mother of God)—that was at the moment of her conception "free from all-stain of sin," by the power of God (Genesis 3:15; Luke 1:28).
[9] Romans 10:9; 1 John 1:9.
[10] John 10:30.
[11] 1 Corinthians 15:12.
[12] John 2:19; 1 Corinthians 6:14.
[13] Mark 16:19.
[14] Acts of Apostles 17:31.
[15] Saint Jerome translated from the Hebrew (Old Testament) text with the exception of Matthew (in Aramaic), for the Greek Septuagint (Old Testament) had errors in it. The Overwhelming majority of the New Testament written in Greek, Saint Jerome translated from the Greek (New Testament).

Saint Pope Damasus I

In 382 A.D., Saint Pope Damasus I (c. 305 – 11th December 384 † A.D.) ordered Saint Jerome (330 – 30th September 420 † A.D.) to revise the *Vetus Latina Vulgata* (Latin: *The Old Latin Vulgate: circa* 157 A.D.). Furthermore, it is the same Pope (mentioned above) that had given us the Books (*Κανών=Kanon=Ruler* in Ancient Greek)[16] of the (Bible=βίβλος in Greek); therefore, the Canon (or Rule) of Holy Scripture was set in place by Saint Pope Damasus I[17] (382 A.D.) Decree[18]; furthermore, it should be noted that Saint Pope Gelasius I (November 21st 496 †

---

[16] ***Giovanni Domenico, Mansi*** (16th February 1692 – 27th September 1769)***: Sacrorum conciliorum nova et amplissima collectio*** (1774 ed.), Vol. 8, pp. 145-147; Cf. ***Patrologia Latina*** by Abbé Minge, Vol. 19, pp. 787-793; See also: ***The Faith of the Early Fathers***, Selected and Translated by W.A. Jurgens, Volume I, Published by Liturgical Press, Collegeville, Minnesota, 1970, Article # 910s-910t, pp. 405-406; Lastly see: (***Decretum Damsi***) ***Enchiridion smybolorum*** by Henrici Denzinger, Editio XLIII (43), Collaborated and Translated by Peter Hunermann and Robert Fastiggi (43rd edition), Published by Ignatius Press, San Francisco, (German ed. 2010; English Edition 2012), Article # 179-180, pp. 70-71.

[17] Pope Damasus I was the 37th Pope of Rome.

[18] Commonly referred to as: ***The Decree of Damasus I*** (382 A.D.) at the Council of Rome.

A.D.) edited the Canon (Bible) of Damasus I making it accepted and authentic rule (Canon)[19] for The Holy Books[20].

From the time of Saint Pope Damasus I (305 – 11th December 384 † A.D.), through the Council of Trent[21] (1545-1563 A.D.), to the present day, the Holy Scriptures (remained as they are) in

---

[19] Cf. The same Canon is given by the Council of Florence – ***Decrees of the Ecumenical Councils,*** Volume One: *Nicaea I to Lateran V*, Edited by Norman P. Tanner, S.J., Published by Sheed & Ward, Georgetown University, 1990, p. 572.

[20] The Council of Trent Decree that: ***Concilium Tridentinum*** (***Council of Trent***: Session IV) April 8th 1546: *First decree: acceptance of the Sacred Books and Apostolic Traditions*; Cf. ***Decrees of the Ecumenical Councils***, Volume Two: Trent to Vatican II, Edited by Norman P. Tanner, S.J., Published by Sheed & Ward, Georgetown University, 1990, pp. 663-664; See also: ***Denzinger*** (The Sources of Catholic Dogma), Translated by Roy J. Deferrari, from the Thirtieth (30th) Edition, Published by B. Herder Book Co., St. Louis, Mo., and London, W.C., 1957, p. 244, Article # 784; See as well: ***Enchiridion smybolorum*** by Henrici Denzinger, Editio XLIII (43), Collaborated and Translated by Peter Hunermann and Robert Fastiggi (43rd edition), Published by Ignatius Press, San Francisco, (German ed. 2010; English Edition 2012), Article # 1502-1505, pp. 370-371; Lastly see: ***The Christian Faith*** edited by Jacques Dupius, Seventh Revised and Enlarged Edition, Published by Alba House, New York, 2001, Article # 211-213, pp. 102-103.

[21] To tamper, interpret, subtract or add to the Canons and Decrees of the Holy Ecumenical 19th Council of the Church (**TRENT**) is evil, scandalous, and heretical. Dear reader, please, in love I write this, the Council of Trent in the person of **Pope Pius IV** ***bulla*** (*bull*) ***Benedictus Deus*** (January 26th 1564) explicitly states: ―Furthermore, in order to avoid the distortion and confusion that could arise if it were permitted to every individual, as he pleased, to publish his own interpretations and commentaries on the decrees of the council: by apostolic authority We order to all ... that none, without Our authorization, should dare to publish any commentaries, glosses, notes, explanations, or any kind of interpretation at all concerning the decrees of the said council or to stipulate anything, by any authority whatsoever, even on the pretext of greater confirmation or execution of the decrees, or for any other exalted reason (***Enchiridion smybolorum by Henrici Denzinger***, Editio XLIII (43), Collaborated and Translated by *Peter Hunermann and Robert Fastiggi* (43rd edition), Published by Ignatius Press, San Francisco, (German ed. 2010; English Edition 2012), Article # 1849, p. 432).

Saint Jerome's Latin-Vulgate. However, in 1965 Antipope Paul VI appointed[22] a commission to "re"-translate the Latin Vulgate—which was completed under Antipope John Paul II in (1979)[23]. For one to believe that the Canon of both (Old & New Testaments) is never-ending in that it is possible that less or more books (be added) or critiques of the Sacred-Scriptures be necessary to be revised from human ingenuity—they are absolutely heretical, evil, and have caused the Greatest-confusion in the world.

---

[22] See the bogus-document from the pseudo-Vatican II (1962-1965) sect ***Sacrosanctum Concilium*** on DECEMBER 4th, 1963, Article # 91.

[23] April 25th 1979, which is called: ***Nova Vulgata Bibliorum Sacrorum Editio—The New Vulgate Edition of the Holy Bible***.

The (heretical) differences between the KJV (1611), Douai-Reims (1582-1610), Douay-Rheims (1749-1752), VS The Holy Latin Vulgate of 1592

Some of the differences (to the eye) are:

"Inimicitias ponam inter te et mulierem et semen tuum et semen illius; ipsum[24] [not ipsa] conteret caput tuum, et tu conteres calcaneum eius—I will put enmity between you and the woman and your seed and her seed; He [not her] will bruise your head, and you will bruise his [not her] heel."[25]

It renders from the KJV[26] (King James Version) 1611[27] Edition as:

---

[24] ***Ipsum*** renders as "He" and not "Her" (***Ipsa***) as in Latin.

[25] Genesis 3:15—***Nova Vulgata Bibliorum Sacrorum Editio—The New Vulgate Edition of the Holy Bible*** 1979, Edition, its rendering as: "He" not "She" will…

[26] ***KJV=King James Verision*** is the same text that has depictions (images) of the Original (1611 ed.) of the King James Version (KJV) of what is believed to be the wood-cuts (at the end of Acts of the Apostles) of Baphomet (the occult deity) & Pan (in Greek mythology)—these wood-cuts (images) are the product of —Sir Francis Bacon (1561 – 1626) who was commissioned by King James I (James Charles Stuart; 1566 – 1625) to make edits to the KJV of whom "both" were Freemasons (Cf. ***The New Free-Mason's Monitor; or Masonic Guide***, by James Hardier, A.M., Published in New York, 1818, p. 7; See also: ***The American Freemason***; A Monthly Masonic Magazine, Volume II., Conducted by Bro. J.F. Brennan, S.P.R.S., Published in New York, 1858, p. 206; ***The Connoisseur***, Volume 64, 1922, Published in London, p. 72). The same King James I was initiated into the Lodge of Freemasonry on: April 15th, 1601. Sir Francis Bacon (22nd January 1561 – 9th April 1626) was "authorized" by Pseudo-King James I to depict (and edit) his bogus-Scriptures with wood-cuts. These most disturbing images (in the Original 1611 Ed. of the KJV) depict freemasonic handshakes and the like as well. He that

"And I will put enmitie betweene thee and the woman, and betweene thy seed and her seed: it [not her] shal bruise thy head, and thou shalt bruise his [not her] heele."[28]

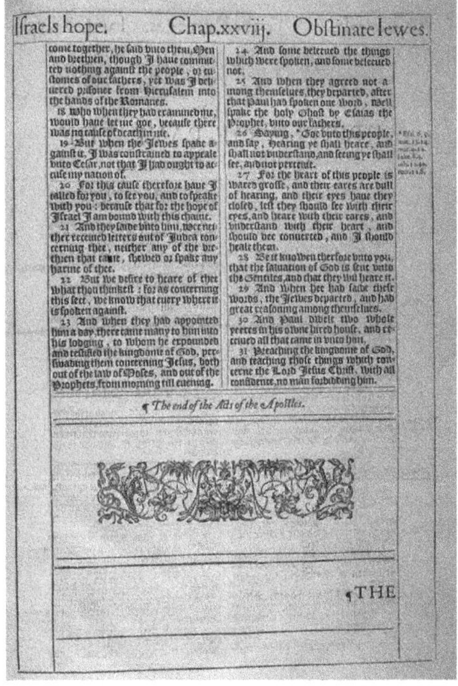

Israels hope. Chap.xxviij. Obstinate Iewes.

come together, he said vnto them, Men
and brethren, though I haue committed nothing against the people, or cu-
stomes of our fathers, yet was I deli-
uered prisoner from Hierusalem into
the hands of the Romanes.
18 Who when they had examined me,
would haue let me goe, because there
was no cause of death in me.
19 But when the Iewes spake a-
gainst it, I was constrained to appeale
vnto Cesar, not that I had ought to ac-
cuse my nation of.
20 For this cause therefore haue I
called for you, to see you, and to speake
with you: because that for the hope of
Israel I am bound with this chaine.
21 And they saide vnto him, Wee neither receiued letters out of Iudea concerning thee, neither any of the brethren that came, shewed or spake any
harme of thee.
22 But we desire to heare of thee
what thou thinkest: for as concerning
this sect, we know that euery where it
is spoken against.
23 And when they had appointed
him a day, there came many to him into
his lodging, to whom he expounded
and testified the kingdome of God, per-
swading them concerning Iesus, both
out of the law of Moses, and out of the
Prophets, from morning till euening.

24 And some beleeued the things
which were spoken, and some beleeued
not.
25 And when they agreed not a-
mong themselues, they departed, after
that Paul had spoken one word, Well
spake the holy Ghost by Esaias the
Prophet, vnto our fathers,
26 Saying, *Goe vnto this people,
and say, Hearing ye shall heare, and
shall not vnderstand, and seeing ye shall
see, and not perceiue.
27 For the heart of this people is
waxed grosse, and their eares are dull
of hearing, and their eyes haue they
closed, lest they should see with their
eyes, and heare with their eares, and
vnderstand with their heart, and
should bee conuerted, and I should
heale them.
28 Be it knowen therefore vnto you,
that the saluation of God is sent vnto
the Gentiles, and that they will heare it.
29 And when hee had saide these
words, the Iewes departed, and had
great reasoning among themselues.
30 And Paul dwelt two whole
yeeres in his owne hired house, and receiued all that came in vnto him,
31 Preaching the kingdome of God,
and teaching those things which con-
cerne the Lord Iesus Christ, with all
confidence, no man forbidding him.

¶ The end of the Acts of the Apostles.

¶ THE

The 1769 Oxford Standardized Revision of the 1611 King James Version (KJV) is what is used by most today! It renders the same verse as:

"And I will put enmity between thee and the woman, and between thy seed and her seed; it [not her] shall bruise thy head, and thou shalt bruise his [not her] heel."[29]

---

believes or condones (*in any way*) the KJV=King James Version—does not have the true Catholic faith (Hebrews 6:4-7) and is outside the Church of Christ (Matthew 18:17) and will be damned to the eternal fires of hell unless before death he seeks reconciliation with the Catholic Church.

[27] The 1611 edition is the "recognized" heretical and dubious-translation of the Holy Scriptures—it is not the Word (Logos) of God.

[28] The damnable (KJV): Genesis 3:15.

[29] Genesis 3:15.

The correct version and translation are found in the (1592 A.D.) Edition of His Holiness of Blessed Memory (Latin: *Clemens VIII*) known as the *Sixti V-Clementi(s)e (VIII)*[30] Edition as follows (based on the *Latin Vulgate* of Saint Jerome):

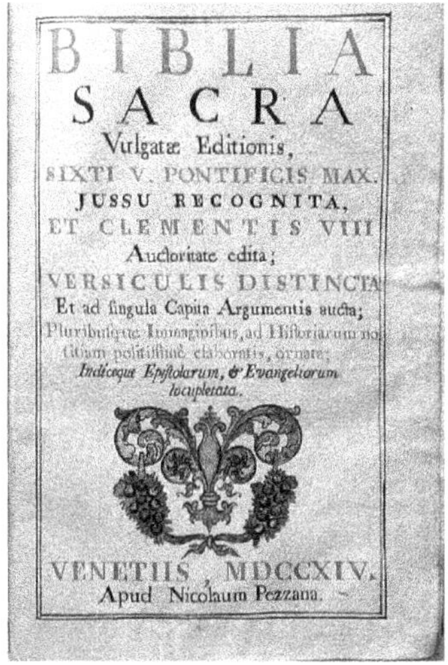
BIBLIA
SACRA
Vulgatæ Editionis,
SIXTI V. PONTIFICIS MAX.
JUSSU RECOGNITA,
ET CLEMENTIS VIII
Auctoritate edita;
VERSICULIS DISTINCTA
Et ad singula Capita Argumentis aucta;
Pluribusque Imaginibus, ad Historiarum no-
titiam politissimè elaboratis, ornata;
Indiceque Epistolarum, & Evangeliorum
locupletata.
VENETIIS, MDCCXIV.
Apud Nicolaum Pezzana.

"Inimicitias ponam inter te et mulierem, et semen tuum et semen illius: ***ipsa***[31] [not *ipsum*=He] conteret caput tuum, et tu insidiaberis calcaneo eius—I will put enmity between thee and the woman, and between thy seed and her seed: she [not He] will crush thy head, and thou wilt be ensnared by her heel"[32]

Another example would be (correctly stated):

---

[30] Otherwise known as: The Sixto-Clementine Vulgate. In addition, His Holiness of Blessed Memory Pope Sixtus V (13th December 1521 – 27th August 1590 † A.D.) decreed a Most Prestigious Document entitled "*Aeternus Illae* (*He is Eternal*, from the Latin)" which preceded (March, 1589) his edition of the Vulgate in (May, 1590 A.D.); furthermore, there were no corrupt text(s) that were deviated from (Sixtus V Vulgate); however, copyist errors (not in Doctrine) but in text were prevalent; therefore, the Vulgate was soon revised by Clement VIII (1592 A.D.) and hence: The Sixto-Clementine Vulgate was the Rule of Faith! Any one that changed or ratified his "own" version(s) of the Sacred Scriptures (the Bible) was deemed "excommunicated, greater" from the Catholic Church—*outside of which there is no salvation nor the remission of sins.*

[31] ***Ipsa***=She in Latin.

[32] Genesis 3:15—The Clementine VIII Edition of the Holy Latin Vulgate (1592); The English Version of the "so-called" Douai-Rheims (1610 A.D.) edition was first published in 1610 while the Douai (Douay) New Testament was published in (1582 A.D.) it renders the same reading as the Clementine (VIII) Vulgate of (1592) as well as the later revisions by Bishop Challoner (1749, 1750, and 1752 A.D) and rendered the same as the above mentioned.

"Qui sedet super ***gyrum*** terrae, et habitatores ejus sunt quasi locustae: qui extendit velut nihilum coelos, ex expandit eos sicut tabernaculum ad inhabitandium—Who sits upon ***the circle*** of the earth, and its inhabitants are like locusts: who stretches out the heavens as nothing, spreads them out like a tent to be inhabited."[33]

This verse[34] above is correct in its form and so forth; however the Reims/Rheims (1610) reads as:

"He that fitteth vpon the compaffe [***compass***=in Latin=***circino***] of the earth, and the inhabitants therof are as locuftes: he that ftretcheth out the heauens as nothing, and fpreddeth them as a tent to dwel in."[35]

---

[33] This is found in the (1592) edition of the Holy Latin Vulgate Bible minor edits by His Holiness of Blessed Memory Pope Clement VIII. However, in the (1991) edition of the Nova Editio (New Edition) of the Clementinam Vulgate the words are rendered the same; therefore, ***Gyrum*** (***Gyrus)***="Circle" in Latin; does not represent, a compass, or globe?

[34] Found within the (1991) edition of the Vulgate; and most notably the Clementine Edition (1592) of Saint Jerome's Latin Vulgate.

[35] Isaie (Isaias/Isaiah) 40:22; Furthermore, the Old Reims/Rheims (1610) edition is incorrect in translating this verse as we shall see in other verses. A Compass is not a Circle (as in the earth) even though it might appear as such it is not.

The Douay-Rheims of Challoner[36] revision has in it (1749-1752)[37]:

"It is he that sitteth upon the globe [the earth is not a globe] of the earth, and the inhabitants thereof are as locusts: he that stretcheth out the heavens as nothing, and spreadeth them out as a tent to dwell in."[38]

Another example is to be found among the KJV (King James Version 1611 edition) of blasphemous writing(s) in this unholy (book) words are as follows:

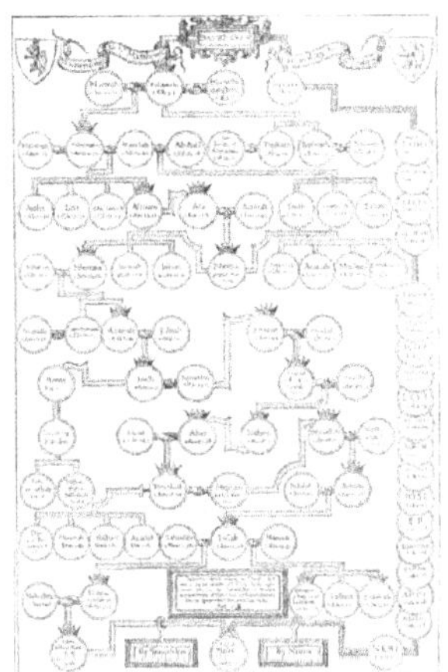

"For thine is the kingdome, and the power, and the glory, for euer, Amen."[39]

---

[36] Bishop Richard Challoner (29 September 1691 – 12 January 1781).

[37] September 1st, 1899 republished by Tan Books and Publishers, Rockford, Illinois, 1971, p. 793.

[38] Isaias (Isaiah) 40:22; Why is this verse in the later edition of the Douay-Rheims without merit in rendering the Holy Latin Vulgate of (1592) invalid? Well, it is uses the world "globe" which "appears" to resemble the World as known by many—not flat (which is justly correct)—however, the word "globe" differs highly from "compass" and in addition, neither are correct, the true word to be used in Latin is: ***Circulus***=Circle, the (1592) edition brings to light this point of Holy Catholic-Doctrine. However, this may seem "minor" to the eye but as further explained it will become clearer to the eye and mind.

[39] The 1611 (Edition) of the KJV (King James Version) adds the words to the Holy Writ (*if it can be called that*) by stating this which is very evil and heretical. For in the Holy Writ of God is it said most sternly that: "*If any man shall add to these things, God shall add unto him the plagues written in this book*" (Apocalypse 22:18). The (Doxology) of these words are not found in the Holy writ (Bible) but added by Protestant-heretics in much later Manuscripts (copies of copies) not the Original or Infallible-sources *per se*. No Protestant has "ever" claimed "Infallibility" and therefore, none can be correct (certain) that they have the Sacred-Scriptures; not like Christ's most Sacred Church, The Catholic Church (Matthew 16:18-19).

Nowhere, in the Holy Writ (Bible) are these words (above) mentioned "whatsoever" but added by Anglican (Protestants) in the early 17th century, that is: "For thine is the kingdome, and the power, and the glory, for euer, Amen."

Christ (God) never said these words (above) and it is evil and vicious (heretical) to read them as if they were true. There is no Protestant (sect) in Heaven, only the Catholic Church and Her alone was the Divine-Scriptures entrusted; and, with Her correct interpretation of them as well; therefore, anything of the Latin Vulgate (1592) edition is true and obedient to the Holy-Words of Christ (God).

Furthermore, and lastly, for now, we turn our attention to these words (erroneously) translated from Latin into English (in the pseudo-Douai/Douay-Rheims editions: 1582/1609) we read:

"Receiue ye the Holy Ghoft: Vvhose Sinnes Yov shal Forgive, They are Forgiven them: And Vvhose Yov Shal Reteine, They Are Reteined."[40]

---

[40] John 20:23; the Douai/Douay (1582/1749-1752) so-called Bible. Furthermore, it is interesting to note that Cardinal Wiseman (3rd August 1802 – 15th February 1865) & Cardinal Newman (21st February 1801 – 11th August 1890)—both with due respect could write on such things, and, about Bishop Challoner's revision being faulty and an abuse; however, when, the very Original Douai-Reims (1582-1610) edition that they cite (came out) it was just as faulty (heretical) as seen above.
Cardinal Wiseman: "—To call it any longer the Douay or Rhemish version is an abuse of terms. It has been altered and modified till scarcely any verse remains as it was originally published; and so far as simplicity and energy of style are concerned, the changes are in general for the worse. For, though Dr. Challoner did well to alter many too decided Latinisms which the old translators had retained, he weakened the language considerably by destroying inversion, where it was congenial, at once, to the genius of our language, and to the construction of the original, and by the insertion of particles where they were by no means necessary. Any chapter of the New Testament will substantiate this remark." (***Dublin Review***, April 1837,

In the Douay-Rheims (Challoner) edition it states (1749-1752):

"Receive ye the Holy Ghost. Whose sins you shall forgive, they are forgiven them; and whose sins you shall retain, they are retained."[41]

However, shockingly, the KJV (King James Version: 1611) reads:

"Receiue ye the holy Ghost. Whose soeuer sinnes yee remit, they are remitted vnto them, and whose soeuer sinnes yee retaine, they are retained."[42]

In the KJV (King James Version) Standard (1769) edition reads:

"Receive ye the Holy Ghost: Whose soever sins ye remit, they are remitted unto them; and whose soever sins ye retain, they are retained."[43]

Lastly, we turn our attention to the Latin Vulgate of St. Jerome found within the (Pope) Clementine VIII Edition of the Holy Latin-Vulgate (1592 A.D.) in these solemn Holy-Words by the Pope of Rome:

Published in London (1853-4?) Volume I, pp. 73-100; Cf. ***The Irish Ecclesiastical Record***, A Monthly Journal, Third Series, Volume I (1880), Article: *A Question Regarding The Hail Mary*, Published in Dublin by Browne & Nolan, 1881, p. 227; See also: ***Tracts Theological and Ecclesiastical*** by **John Henry Cardinal Newman**, Published by Longmans, Green, And Co., in London, 1913, p. 416; See also: ***The Biblical World***, Editor in Chief Ernest De Witt Burton, New Series Vol. XXXVII [37], January--June, 1911, Published by The University of Chicago Press, Chicago, Illinois, p. 244, see footnotes; Lastly see: ***Papal Vacancy*** (2023) by William DeTucci (footnotes 70 &71) pp. 46-47.

[41] John 20:23; the Douay-Rheims (Challoner revision) 1749-1752 edition.

[42] John 20:23, the King James Version (1611 original).

[43] John 20:23; the King James Version (1769) Oxford Standardized Revision.

"Accipite Spiritum Sanctum: quorum remiseritis peccata, remittuntur eis : et quorum retinueritis, retenta sunt."[44]

Translated (Literally) as:

"Receive ye the Holy Ghost. Whosoever sins ye remit, they are remitted unto them, and whosoever sins ye retain, they are retained."[45]

---

[44] Secundum Ioannem (The Gospel According to John); Ioannem 20:23 (or) John 20:23); the Clementine (VIII) Edition of the Holy Latin Vulgate (1592 A.D.).

[45] John 20:23; translation of the Holy-Scriptures of God (The Blessed Trinity). Furthermore, why is this "text" utterly important to get "correct"? Why? For one, Christ (God) stated to men that they would not be "forgiven" their sins unless they "forgave" their enemies/neighbors, etc. in Matthew 6:12. Men (fallible) could receive "forgiveness" from their sins (unless they truly forgave those that sinned against them); on this account by Christ (God) Himself; however, men (did not) have the Authority as the Apostles did to "retain" sins; therefore, "only" the Apostles (of God-Christ) and their true and legitimate-successors had such an Authority to REMIT or RETAIN THE SINS of Men! 2nd only the Catholic Church (Christ's Church) in Her capacity as Mother and Teacher is "Infallible" and endowed with *the charism* of Infallibility—that is Her Popes (Roman Pontiffs), etc. No one at any time has claimed to be "infallible" or animated from Christ (God); only the Catholic Church (Matthew 16:18-19) is the Ark of Eternal Salvation (Matthew 18:17; 1 Peter 3:20) and Her (The Catholic Church) alone (John 16:13)!

Obviously there is a major-discrepancy among these varied translation(s)[46] of the True Holy-Bible (The Latin Vulgate) of Pope Clement VIII (1592)[47]. Therefore, he that resists (rejects) the Sacred and Canonical Texts (of the Bible) and all their Parts[48]—are condemned to the fires of Hell[49], unless, before death, he is truly-untied (reconciled) to the Catholic Church. Only that Source is "Infallible"[50] that has the *Charism* of Infallibility[51] from God (Christ)[52]. Therefore, Christ and His Catholic Church are One[53] and the Same[54]!

---

[46] The Douai/Douay & Reims/Rheims are "not" the Word of God in the strict sense; they have "mis"-translated words in them (their texts) and are faulty thereof. Only the Latin Vulgate (1592 A.D.) is Infallible and the Word of God as defined by Pope Clement VIII in the Papal bull ***Cum Sacrorum*** (*With the Sacred*) of 9th November 1592 A.D.
[47] The Papal Bull, in Latin: ***Cum Sacrorum—With the Sacred***, published on November 9th 1592 A.D., the pseudo-Catholic Church (replaced this text in 1979).
[48] The Council of Trent (Session 4, April 8th 1546 A.D.); Cf. ***Decrees of the Ecumenical Councils***, Volume Two: Trent to Vatican II, Edited by Norman P. Tanner, S.J., Published by Sheed & Ward, Georgetown University, 1990, p. 664. "*If anyone should not accept as sacred and canonical these entire books and all their parts as they have, by established custom, been read in the catholic church, and as contained in the old Latin Vulgate edition, and in conscious judgment should reject the aforesaid traditions:* ***let him be anathema***."
[49] The Papal Bull ***Cantate Domino*** (February 4th 1442 A.D.), of Pope Eugene IV, at the Council of Florence; Cf. ***Decrees of the Ecumenical Councils,*** Volume One: *Nicaea I to Lateran V*, Edited by Norman P. Tanner, S.J., Published by Sheed & Ward, Georgetown University, 1990, p. 578; See also: ***Denzinger*** (The Sources of Catholic Dogma), Translated by Roy J. Deferrari, from the Thirtieth (30th) Edition, Published by B. Herder Book Co., St. Louis, Mo., and London, W.C., 1957, p. 230, Article # 714; Cf. ***Enchiridion smybolorum*** by Henrici Denzinger, Editio XLIII (43), Collaborated and Translated by Peter Hunermann and Robert Fastiggi (43rd edition), Published by Ignatius Press, San Francisco, (German ed. 2010; English Edition 2012), p. 348, Article # 1351.
[50] John 16:13.
[51] Luke 10:16.
[52] God and Christ are ONE! 1 Colossians 1:16: "For in him were all things created in heaven and on earth, visible and invisible, whether thrones, or dominations, or principalities, or powers: all things were created by him and in him." God the Son was NOT created—but CREATED—the Angels, (Satan, etc.).

For example, we read the Epistle's of Saint Paul the following:

"And to whom you have pardoned [Latin: donastis] any thing, I also. For, what I have pardoned [Latin: donavi], if I have pardoned [Latin: donavi] any thing, for your sakes have I done it *in the person of Christ*."[55] (Emphasis mine).

However the KJV (King James Version) reads not "Pardon" but "forgive" and is clearly wrong (heretical) on this point; however, it does state in the text that: "In the Person of Christ." Saint Paul not only "Pardoned" the offense (sin) but he did it "not" in the "presence"[56] of Christ, however, "*In the Person of Christ—In Persona Christi* (in Latin)."

Furthermore, we can see the discrepancy (heresies) in this passage of Sacred Scripture from the Apostle Saint John (100-101 † A.D) Epistle, as follows:

---

[53] 1 Corinthians 12:12.

[54] Matthew 16:18; Matthew 18:17; John 1:42; Acts of the Apostles 20:28; Ephesians 2:20.

[55] 2 Corinthians 2:10.

[56] In addition the so-called RSV (Revised Standard Version) Catholic Edition (# 2) has in it (2 Cor. 2:10): "in the presence of Christ."—trying to water-down—true Catholic Doctrine and to deny the Sacred Scriptures (The Vulgate Bible of 1592 A.D.). Many so-called "re"-visions or versions of the Sacred Scriptures (maligned by heretics) have the same wording as well—beware of these imposter-scriptures.

"If vve confeffe our finnes: he is faithful & iuft, for to forgive [Correct Latin Word: *Remittat*—Remit][57] vs out finnes, and to cleanfe vs from al iniguitie."[58]

"If we confess our sins, he is faithful and just, to forgive [Correct Latin Word: *Remittat*—Remit] us our sins, and to cleanse us from all iniquity."[59]

For this reason the Apostle Saint Peter (64 † A.D.)[60] teaches:

---

[57] The Confession of Sins implies that one (understands) and confesses his sins (according to his conscience) and therefore one is Sacramentally-Baptized for there would be no need to "remit" the sin—if we confess our sins to the priest who represents God. Please do keep in mind that one must be baptized in order to receive the *remission of his sins* from Christ (God). Therefore, does the Douai/Douay (1582 & 1749-1752 editions) correctly translate this passage of Sacred Scripture—no they do not! We can see this based upon the Clementine Vulgate (1592).

[58] 1 John 1:9; the (1582) Douai-Rheims (Reims) Version has in it.

[59] 1 John 1:9; the Douay-Rheims (1749-1752) also known as the Challoner (Bishop) revision is the word "Forgive used; while the true Bible (The Latin Vulgate) of 1592 under Pope Clement VIII (1592 Vulgate) has in the same passage: "remittat" (Latin=remits). The pseudo-KJV (King James Version) follows in the same guise as the-heretical Douai/Douay on this passage of Sacred Scripture. Lastly, in The New Strong's Exhaustive Concordance of the Bible by James Strong (1822-1894), Published (1995/1996) by Thomas Nelson Publishers, Nashville, TN., p. 1118 (Hardcover edition); never is the word "Remission" mentioned throughout the Old Testament, not even once!

[60] Saint Peter (The First True-Pope) Matthew 16:18-19 of whom he had his name changed by Christ (God) from *Simon* (Aramaic: שִׁמְעוֹן*—to listen or to hear) to Rock* (Aramaic: *Cephas/Kephas=Massive Bedrock)* in (John 1:42) in Greek (*Πέτρος*) it would be ***Petros*** (a masculine noun for a masculine name). Furthermore, the Church (Catholic) that Christ-God had promised to Build (Matthew 16:18-19) His Church upon the "Rock"=Peter is the Catholic Church—*outside of which there is neither salvation nor the remission of sins* (Cf. the Papal Bull of His Holiness of Blessed Memory Pope Boniface VIII (1303 † A.D.) in ***Unam Sanctam*** (November 18th 1302 A.D.); Lastly see: ***Denzinger*** (The Sources of Catholic Dogma), Translated by Roy J. Deferrari, from the Thirtieth (30th) Edition, Published by B. Herder Book Co., St. Louis, Mo., and London, W.C., 1957, p. 186, Article # 468.

"As also in all his epistles [Saint Paul], speaking in them of these things; in which are certain things hard to be understood, which the unlearned and unstable wrest, as they do also the other scriptures, to their own destruction."[61]

The above are just some different examples of why "words" matter and their importance. Moving on to an earlier point the reason(s) the World (Earth) is not a compass or a globe is that neither accurately displays the Earth. God in His mysteries has revealed to us in the Latin Vulgate (1592) the meaning of this word as being "circle." However why cannot the word Globe (in a sense represents a circle or compass be used indicating a circle)? Well, a Globe is a three-dimensional object used to fool and trick people into why the World (Earth) is not flat? A Compass indicates direction and acts in the same way as a Globe, etc. The Correct answer is a Circle as the (1592) Vulgate states it is. Why a Circle? What about the four (4) corners of the Earth and the Angels? In the Apocalypse it I stated:

"Post haec vidi quattuor angelos stantes super quattuor angulos [Latin: angles] terrae tenentes quattuor ventos terrae ne flaret ventus super terram neque super mare neque in ullam arborem—[Translation

---

[61] 2 Peter 3:16.

mine] After these things, I saw four angels standing on the four angles of the earth, holding the four winds of the earth, that they should not blow upon the earth nor upon the sea nor on any tree."[62]

Furthermore, an "angle" could possibly be something rounded (as in a coffee-table) or a night-stand (or something other piece of furniture or object, etc.). In addition, (not that I am guessing but using the argument that) the Author (Saint John the Apostle) has written that (possibly) with Metaphoric-Language (that is) Figurative (Language) in this passage of Sacred Scripture. We do not know, but accept it with Faith, Hope, and Charity in this demonic-like world of today and yesteryear (the past)!

However, the Sacred Scriptures do not identify necessarily with "corners"[63] but rather with "angles". Furthermore, the word "Apocalypse (means) = *end of the world*" the word "Revelation" does not mean the same as "Apocalypse" but rather to "reveal" or "unclothe" something to: "*reveal that which is hidden*". Therefore, they are very different words with different meanings? The pseudo-Orthodox[64] uses the KJV (King James Version) in their sect(s) of

---

[62] Apocalypse 7:1; Cf. Daniel 7:2-5.

[63] Both the (1610) edition of the Douay-Reims and the Douay-Rheims (1749-52) editions have within it—corners as well unlike the Latin Vulgate (1592 A.D.) of His Holiness Pope Clement VIII.

[64] This sect of perdition uses the so-called *New King James Version*—(*NKJV*) text throughout: **The Orthodox Study Bible**: *Ancient Christianity Speaks to Today's World*, Prepared under the auspices of the Academic Community of St. Athanasius Academy of orthodox Theology, Elk Grove, California, General Editor: Fr. Peter E. Gillquist, Published by Thomas Nelson Publishing Company, Nashville, TN., New Testament Text & Citations from: New King James Version (NKJV), 2008 (cf. Older edition 1993).

(heretical) depravity and this is (an) introduction into Protestantism (the Founder not Martin Luther, but the Devil himself). Therefore, every sect (of religion or no religion) is of the Devil[65] other than the Catholic Church (Matthew 16:18-19)[66] which is of Christ (God). He that follows or believes in the pseudo-Teachings of these so-called men[67] worships in reality the Devil and his minions[68]. Therefore, and with caution do we take-care (in this life) to not believe (teach) or follow the sins (heresies) of these so-called sects of (depression) and heretical-perdition. In addition, the so-called Vatican II (1962-1965)[69] sect of perdition is of the Devil (Satan)[70] and his minions of hell[71],

---

[65] John 8:44.

[66] Furthermore, it is highly to be noted that (St.) Papias of Hierapolis (60-130 † A.D., now modern day Turkey) was a disciple of Saint John the Evangelist; Eusebius of Caesarea (or known also as: *Pamphilius*) in his Ecclesiastical History (Book III=3, Chapter 39), writes that Papias knew that Matthew wrote in Hebrew (or Aramaic) the Language of Jesus at this time, in his Gospel.

[67] Caiaphas/Caiphas (*died* 46 A.D.); Annas/Ananus or Ananias (his death is unknown possible suggestions have been are around 40 A.D.); Pontius Pilatus/Pilate (died 36 A.D); Herod-Antipas (39 A.D.); (Muhammad/Mohammed *died* 8th June 632); Photios/Photius (*died* 6th February 893); Michael C(K)erularius (*died* 21st January 1059); Mark of Ephesus/Eugenikos (*died* June 23rd, 1444); John Hus (*died* 6th July 1415); John Wycliffe (*died* 31st December 1384); Martin Luther (*died* 18th February 1546); Ulrich Zwingli (*died* 11th October 1531); Henry VIII (*died* 28th January 1547) ; Mahatma Gandhi (*died* 30th January 1948), etc…

[68] Matthew 12:24; 25:41.

[69] Neither (Never) were the so-called claimants to the Papacy ever "truly" inducted into the Catholic Church (the last true Pope was His Holiness Pope Pius XII † 1958): John XXIII (1958-1963); Paul VI (1963-1978); John Paul I (1978-1978); John Paul II (1978-2005); Benedict XVI (2005-2013); Francis (2013—present) are, were and will always be Antipopes that secured "their" pseudo-Office(s) by way of manipulation. The True (Catholic) Church is eclipsed at present moment however She (The Church) shines ever so bright with Correct Doctrine (Teaching).

[70] 2 Thessalonians 2:9-10; Apocalypse 20:9-10.

[71] Matthew 7:21-25. Christ (God) is the Wise (Man) that built His House (Church) not upon sand but upon *Peter=the Rock* (John 1:42) of the Church (Matthew 16:18).

apostasy[72], and eternal-death[73]! He that has "ears" let him listen (hear)[74]!

Lastly, we read from the Gospel of Saint Luke[75] (The Physician):

"Et cœperunt cogitare scribæ et pharisæi, dicentes: Quis est hic, qui loquitur blasphemias? quis potest dimittere peccata, nisi solus Deus?—[Translation mine] And the scribes and Pharisees began to think, saying: Who is this who speaketh blasphemies? Who can ***release*** [dismiss] sins, but God alone?"[76] (Emphasis mine).

Furthermore, the KJV (King James Version: 1611 edition) reads the above text as thus:

"And the Scribes and the Pharisees began to reason, saying, Who is this which speaketh blasphemies? Who can forgiue sinnes, but God alone?"[77]

---

[72] Judas Iscariot (Matthew 26:14) was an Apostate from the True Faith (Catholic) and died and went to hell; not that we should "ever" wish or want this upon any man at any time; but the reality is that Judas Iscariot fell into the sin of despair—he thought his sin was so great that even Christ (God) according to Judas could not forgive or (remit) him of his (Judas') sins. Never, I beg you, fall into the sin of "despair" God can do all things (Luke 18:27)—man cannot (without the aid of God and He and He Alone).

[73] Apocalypse 2:11; 20:6; 20:14; 21:8.

[74] Matthew 11:15; 13:9; 13:43; Mark 4:9; Luke 8:8.

[75] Saint Luke was born between 1 A.D. and/or 16 A.D. – 84 A.D. and/or 100 A.D., traditionally he is said to have died at 84 years old.

[76] Luke 5:21; The Holy Latin Vulgate Bible 1592 (ed.).

[77] Luke 5:21; the KJV (King James Version 1611 ed.).

In the 1769 Oxford Standardized Revision of the KJV we read as follows:

"And the scribes and the Pharisees began to reason, saying, Who is this which speaketh blasphemies? Who can forgive sins, but God alone?"[78]

In the Douai (1582 edition) it is stated:

"And the Scribes and Pharisees began to thinke, saying: Who is this that speaketh blasphemies? Who can foriue sinnes, but only God?"[79]

In the Douay revised (1749-1752) by Bishop Challoner it is written:

"And the scribes and Pharisees began to think, saying: Who is this who speaketh blasphemies? Who can forgive sins, but God alone?"[80]

Thus we can surely (with certainty) compare the texts against the Vulgate (Latin) and each of these (pseudo) texts is invalid, worthless, and heretical as well. Even in the pseudo-Douai/Douay-Reims/Rheims versions there are major "interpolations, mistranslations, etc." when compared to the Latin Vulgate of 1592[81]. The correct rendering of the word: "dimittere" is to: "release or dimiss" not to "forgive."

---

[78] Luke 5:21; the KJV (King James Version 1769 ed.).
[79] Luke 5:21; the Douai (1582 ed.).
[80] Luke 5:21; the Douay (1749-1752 ed.).
[81] The Holy Latin Vulgate Bible 1592 is the set-standard of the Roman Catholic Church; and, the faith thereof. Any text (for the Latin Church) is utterly null, void, and useless.

Surely we can trace back the Origins of these errors (heresies) to the Jews[82] and their interpolations/mistranslation(s) of the Divine-Texts at hand. But the true and real Author[83] of these fallacies (lies) and evil is of the Devil (Satan) himself the father of all lies[84] and heresies. The Jews (those circumcised[85] and follow the Old-Testament-laws and rituals) are damned (anathematized) to hell and will never see the light of God in His Kingdom forever unless before death the Jew(s) are converted to Christ[86], embrace the true Catholic Faith[87], and receive the Sacrament of Holy Baptism[88].

---

[82] Matthew 28:13-15; Cf. ***Destroy the Holy Sacrament of Baptism and you have Destroyed the Catholic Church*** by William DeTucci (2024).

[83] *Lucifer=Light Bearer* (Isaias 14:12) is the source of all evil, etc.

[84] John 8:44.

[85] There is no sect(s) (of a false-religion(s) in Heaven) the Only Church that will remain for all eternity will be the Catholic Church; never will there be a Church of the (circumcised) and one of the (baptized); however, all in Heaven will have been Baptized beforehand or entrance into the Kingdom of God (John 3:5)—no one can be saved following (and dying) in the Old-Mosaic Law(s), Custom(s), and Ritual(s); therefore, all prior entry into the Kingdom of God will be by profess the True Faith (Catholic) and be Baptized (Sacramentally) and will pass Purgatory (through its fires) unless released/died (in the state of Sanctifying Grace); therefore, those that die with only Venial sin(s) on their souls (but hopeful) will be tried (by fire) till they reach the state of Sanctifying Grace.

[86] Christ (God) is One Person but with two natures: Divine and human; He is the *Messiah (Latin: Messiam/Messias)=The Anointed One=Christ* (John 1:4, 4:25); according to Holy Scripture there are only two places in the New Testament that make reference to the Messiah; Cf. ***Encyclopedic dictionary of the Bible*** *A translation and adaptation of A. van den Born's Bijbels woordenboek*, 2d rev. ed., 1954-1957 (Published by Usines Brepols, S.A., in Belgium), Translated (in English) and Published by McGraw-Hill Book Company, INC., 1963, New York, p. 1509.

[87] Matthew 18:17; If the Jew does not even listen (or hear/believe) the Church; he will be damned forever.

[88] John 3:5.

Lastly, we see Christ (God) in His human nature call upon God the Father to "release" them from their sins (Luke 23:34) for they do not know what they do.

"Jesus autem dicebat: Pater, dimitte [*release*] illis: non enim sciunt quid faciunt."[89]

The Reims version (1582) has in it:

"And IESVS said: Father, forgiue them, for they know not what they doe."

The Rheims (Challoner) edition (1749-1752) has in it:

"And Jesus said: Father, forgive them, for they know not what they do."

Furthermore, why is this passage of Sacred-Scripture so important? Well, to begin God (Christ) had not died on the Cross (as of yet), Rose from the Dead[90], and Ascended[91] to Heaven. In addition, the Gentile-Soldiers of who Christ spoke about were those that were "not" Baptized (received the Full remission of their sins)[92]. Christ (God) "prayed to His Heavenly-Father" to "release them (the Gentile-Soldiers)"[93] from their sins, etc. In addition, to be "ignorant" (not in

---

[89] Luke 23:34; The Holy Latin Vulgate Bible of 1592 by His Holiness of Blessed Memory Pope Clement VIII contains the true Words of God (The Blessed Trinity)—Three Divine Persons—yet One True Eternal God. Unity in Trinity, Trinity in Unity!

[90] Luke 24:6-7.

[91] Luke 24:51.

[92] The true and only "exception" to this rule is: The Holy Mother of God (Luke 1:28) who was Baptized (not to remove sin[s], she had none); however, to become a Member of the Church (Catholic) and to receive the Sacramental seal (sign) upon her-soul and to receive her-Son (Christ/God) in Holy-Communion.

[93] Luke 23:34; John 19:24.

all cases) is a sin (crime) against Christ (God)[94] and His Holy Catholic Church[95]—thoughts[96] are sins[97]—even if we are "ignorant" of the Law of God (written on the Hearts of men)[98]; actions are much graver in comparison[99]. For this reason not only will the soul suffer in Hell (if we go there sadly) but the Pains of Hell will come (as well) when the Resurrection of the body[100] will be united to the soul—even more torments await those that die in Original[101] or Mortal sin[102].

Therefore, it is the Jews[103] that have denied (doubted) and despaired about Christ (God); it is He alone that can save men from their sin(s) by Water and the Holy Ghost (John 3:5). Without the Blessed Trinity[104] *there is absolutely no eternal-salvation*—founded only within the true Catholic Church (Matthew 16:18-19). Christ (God) "promised" to be with His Church till the end and rightly so; however, heretics and the like (the Jews) have caused the greatest disunity (never prevailing against the Church, Catholic) but eclipsing that which is replicated[105] in its place.

---

[94] John 1:1.
[95] Matthew 16:18.
[96] Matthew 5:28.
[97] James 4:17; one is excused from sin (mortal) in (infants, retards—those with mental challenges, and one that does something that which is not on the higher grades of the Catholic Truths; for example missing (intentionally) Mass on a Sunday obligation.
[98] Romans 2:14-15; 2 Corinthians 3:2-3.
[99] Galatians 5:19-21.
[100] Matthew 10:28.
[101] Romans 5:12; the clear and precise two-souls that never committed or were conceived in Original (sin) are: Christ (God); and His Holy Mother (Mary); Saint Joseph was conceived in Original sin (but as I can see he never committed a Mortal or Venial sin—ever!).
[102] 1 John 5:16-17.
[103] Matthew 28:12-15.
[104] Matthew 28:19; 1 John 5:7.
[105] There is only "One True Catholic Church" and to try (even though) it may "appear" to be: with the bells and whistles—it will never be the Catholic Church.

To make it clear to all, and pristine let us make our doctrinal works known now: Only Christ (God) and His Holy Mother (Mary) were *never* conceived in Original sin(s) and for that matter they neither committed in thought, word, deed, or omitted "anything" at any time concerning Original, Mortal, or Venial Sin(s). In order for Christ (the Precious Lamb of God)[106] to accomplish His Mission He needed (and wanted) to only do the Heavenly Father's Will—which He did "infinitely" by dying on the Cross (not as God) but as man—the "soul" of Christ would live on like that to men[107], that depart this life. Christ (God) cannot die but his human (physical nature) did die but not his soul like all men. The Holy Mother of God never needed to be cleansed from sin(s)[108] at all at any time; However, She (the most beautiful of God's Creation) was in need of Water and the Holy Ghost (John 3:5)—again, not to wash away sin; however, to make her a member of Christ's Mystical Body (His Church)[109]. Therefore, Mary, Most-Holy, in addition, received the Sacrament (indelible) of Confirmation prior (before)[110] she was assumed into Heaven Body and Soul[111]. Therefore, and lastly, to receive her Divine Son (Christ) in Holy-Communion (The Eucharist) in the Holy Sacrifice of the Mass.

When someone wants a true genuine Rolex-watch—they want the "real" thing and not an *imitation*!

[106] John 1:29, 1:36.

[107] Genesis 2:7; John 5:28-29.

[108] Luke 1:28; Mary was "Full of Grace" at her Conception.

[109] Mary the Mother of Christ (God) received Holy Communion (Her Divine Son) in the Holy Eucharist=Perfectly.

[110] It is the Author's *opinion* that the Holy Mother of God did *not die* but went to sleep and now she is with God in Heaven both Body and Soul.

[111] APOSTOLIC CONSTITUTION OF *POPE PIUS XII* ***MUNIFICENTISSIMUS DEUS*** DEFINING THE DOGMA OF THE ASSUMPTION November 1st, 1950, Article # 44. Please do keep in mind that Pope Pius XII never defined whether Mary

The Canon of Scripture has been "defined"[112] by the Catholic Church since: 382 A.D. by His Holiness of Blessed Memory Saint Pope Damasus (I) at the Council of Rome. Therefore, any "new" or existing manuscripts are deemed invalid, and worthless. The Pope (Damasus I) decided back in 382 A.D. as the definition of the Sacred-Scriptures. It must be utterly (absolutely) that Pope (Damasus I) *defined* the Sacred-Scriptures at the (Council of Rome) to the known world and to pursue any further is tantamount of Heresy. The conclusion then is that the Canon (Rule) of the Sacred-Books has been defined by an *infallible-authority*[113]. Therefore, any manuscripts either existing prior (382 A.D.) or thereafter are invalid and worthless unless they were attributed and bound by the Infallible Word (God) Himself[114] in the Sacred-Writers of the Holy-Scriptures. No pseudo-Orthodox sect of perdition dares state at any time that "anyone" is infallible[115] in their sect of perdition (even if all) come together and "supposedly" hold a Council it is absolutely invalid unless it be

---

had died or not, therefore the only thing he (Pope Pius XII, defined) was: "*expleto terrestris vitae—completed her earthly life*" (Article #44).

[112] ***Giovanni Domenico, Mansi*** (16th February 1692 – 27th September 1769): ***Sacrorum conciliorum nova et amplissima collectio*** (1774 ed.), Vol. 8, pp. 145-147; Cf. ***Patrologia Latina*** by Abbé Minge, Vol. 19, pp. 787-793; See also: ***The Faith of the Early Fathers***, Selected and Translated by W.A. Jurgens, Volume I, Published by Liturgical Press, Collegeville, Minnesota, 1970, Article # 910t, p. 406; Lastly see: (***Decretum Damsi***) ***Enchiridion smybolorum*** by Henrici Denzinger, Editio XLIII (43), Collaborated and Translated by Peter Hunermann and Robert Fastiggi (43rd edition), Published by Ignatius Press, San Francisco, (German ed. 2010; English Edition 2012), Article # 179-180, pp. 70-71.

[113] The Roman Pontiff (Matthew 16:18-19) is "infallible" on Faith and Morals of the Catholic Church; who has Christ (God) as His guide and the Holy Ghost (God) as its Teacher; therefore, the Catholic Church cannot fail us at any time or any place.

[114] The Latin Vulgate (1592) *without question* is equal (with all its parts) to that of the Original Texts by the Authors of the Holy-Scriptures.

[115] Cf. the Book ***Heterodox or Orthodox*** (2023) by William J. DeTucci.

approved or from the Roman Pontiff(s) themselves. In hindsight as well are the so-called Protestants (shipwreck) and without the true-faith as well; no one has ever claimed infallibility in their sect of perdition. Therefore they will be judged by Christ and deemed worthy of the eternal-flames of hell if they die in that state. Furthermore, the Decree of Saint Pope Damasus I (in 382 A.D) was later ratified by the Council of Florence[116] (1431-1445 A.D.) and the Council of Trent[117] (1545-1563 A.D.) as well.

Many counterfeits (sects) have been produced[118] over the years (by Satan and his minions) using men to be the instruments of their mayhem to deceive even the elect[119] of God. However, only in the Catholic Church is there *eternal-salvation*; in Her alone is the fountain of eternal-life and peace found.

---

[116] ***Denzinger*** (The Sources of Catholic Dogma), Translated by Roy J. Deferrari, from the Thirtieth (30th) Edition, Published by B. Herder Book Co., St. Louis, Mo., and London, W.C., 1957, pp. 33-34, Article # 84; Cf. ***Decrees of the Ecumenical Councils***, Volume One: Nicaea I to Lateran V, Edited by Norman P. Tanner, S.J., Published by Sheed & Ward, Georgetown University, 1990, p. 572.

[117] ***Decrees of the Ecumenical Councils***, Volume Two: Trent to Vatican II, Edited by Norman P. Tanner, S.J., Published by Sheed & Ward, Georgetown University, 1990, pp. 663-664.

[118] Man-made sects that absolutely were not founded by God (Christ) but by the Devil and his minions; that is: manufactured.

[119] Mark 13:22.

The Pope of Rome has NO RIGHT to Tamper with the True Catholic Faith

Saint Paul (Koinē Greek: *Παῦλος*, romanized: *Paûlos*) the Apostle (64/65 † A.D.) writes:

"But though we [Pope or bishops/clergy/ or any man], or an angel from heaven, preach a gospel to you besides that which we have preached to you, let him be anathema [accursed]. As we said before, so now I say again: If any one preach to you a gospel, besides that which you have received, let him be anathema [accursed]. For do I now persuade men, or God? Or do I seek to please men? If I yet pleased men, I should not be the servant of Christ."[120]

Pope Innocent III (1160-1216 † A.D.) in Sermon Two[121] on the Priestly Office teaches:

"In fact, unless I am grounded in faith, how can I make others firm in faith? It is certain that faith belongs especially to my office. The Lord publicly pro-claimed it: I, 'He said, have prayed for thee, Peter, that thy faith may not fail, and thee, once being converted, must confirm thy brothers (Luke 22:32).' He asked, and he received, because He was

---

[120] Galatians 1:8-10.

[121] Innocent III composed this sermon for the occasion of his consecration as Bishop of Rome, February 22nd, 1198, the Feast of St. Peter's Chair at Antioch, six weeks after his election as Pope (8th January 1198 A.D.); Cf. the book ***Papal Vacancy*** by William J. DeTucci (2023), p. 175.

heard in all things by virtue of his reverence (Hebrews 5:7). 'For that reason the faith of the apostolic seat has never failed even during turbulent times, but has remained whole and unharmed, so that the privilege of Peter continues to be unshaken. So necessary is faith for me as Pope, that, while I have God alone as the judge of my other sins, I can be judged by the church only for any sin committed against the Faith. For he who does not believe, is already judged (John 3:18). 'I believe—I most certainly believe—what I may believe as a Catholic, confident that my faith is bound to save me just as the promise says, Your faith has saved you. Go, and sin no more (Luke 8:48; John 8:11).' "[122]

---

[122] ***Source***: Sermon II of ***Patrologia Latina***, Vol. 217: p. 656; cf. ***Pope Innocent III Between God & Man Six Sermons on the Priestly Office***, by Corrine J. Vause and Frank C. Gardiner, Published by Catholic University America Press, Washington D.C., 2004, pp. 21-22; Also see: ***Conciliarism and Papalism***, Edited by: J.H. Burns, Published by: Cambridge University Press, 1997, p. 116; See also: ***The Christian Tradition*** by Jaroslav Pelikan, Volume 4, Reformation of Church and Dogma (1300-1700), Published by University of Chicago Press, 1984, p. 107; See also: ***Catholic Statements****: Christ and His Teachings* by William J. DeTucci Published in 2021, p. 79; Lastly see: ***Papal Vacancy*** by William J. DeTucci (2023), p. 176.

Citations from St. Jerome

"Ignoratio Scripturarum ignoratio Christi est.—Ignorance of Scripture is ignorance of Christ."[123]

"He who is not arguing is not married."[124]

---

[123] ***Patrologia Latina*** Volume 24, p. 17; Cf. The Papal Encyclical of Pope Benedict XV, ***SPIRITUS PARACLITUS*** September 15, 1920, the Latin text has note: # 132 as opposed to the English translation of # 121; Cf. In Is., Prol.; cf. tract. de Ps. 77; Lastly see: ***The First Book of The Commentary on Isaiah by St. Jerome Priest***, Ancient Christian Writers (ACW), Translated with Introduction by Thomas P. Scheck, (Number 68), Published by The Newman Press (Paulist Press), New York/Mahwah, NJ., 2015, p. 67.

[124] ***Patrologia Latina*** Volume 23, p. 261; Cf. ***Adv. Jov.***, *lib. I, n. 28*; See lastly: ***The Theology of Marriage*** *The Historical Development of Christian Attitudes Toward Sex and Sanctity in Marriage* by Joseph E. Kerns, S.J., Published by Sheed and Ward in New York, 1964, p. 143.

"As I follow no leader save Christ, so I communicate with none but thy blessedness, that is with the chair of Peter. For this, I know, is the Rock on which the Church is built 'Matthew 16:18'! This is the house [Ark] where alone the paschal lamb can be rightly eaten 'Exodus 12:22'. This is the Ark of Noah, and he who is not found in it shall perish when the flood prevails '(Genesis 7:23)'. "[125]

[125] Letter 15, Chapter 2; Cf. The Papal Encyclical Letter ***SPIRITUS PARACLITUS*** of Pope Benedict XV, September 15, 1920, Article # 68; See also: ***The Nicene and Post-Nicene Fathers*** (Volume VI) *Letters and Select Works* (Second Series) Translated by W.H. Fremantle, Published originally by (T&T Clark in Edinburgh) cited version by WM. B. Eerdmans Publishing Company, Grand Rapids, Michigan, Reprinted 1996, pp. 18; See also: ***Ancient Christian Writers, The Letters of St. Jerome*** (Volume I), Number 33 in Series Translated by Charles Christopher Mierow, Published by Newman Press, New York, N.Y., and Mahwah, N.J., 1963, p.71; Lastly see: ***The Rise of the Papacy*** by Robert B. Eno, Theology and Life Series (Number 32), Published by Michael Glazier, Inc., Wilmington, Delaware, 1990, p. 85.

1 John 5:7 Comma Johanneum

Johannine Comma (Latin: *Comma Johanneum*)—(translation mine):

John's Comma—or *The Comma of John*. In the Latin Vulgate this verse is absolutely present (from Saint Jerome[126] to the Present 1592 edition of the Vulgate) and to take it out or water-it-down or despise it will be unimaginable the unending-torments—"And if anyone diminishes the words of the book of this prophecy, God will take away his part from the book of life, and from the holy city, and from the things that are written in this book."[127]

---

[126] Saint Jerome was fluent in Hebrew (from the Jew Baraninas) in Bethlehem, Cf. Letter LXXXIV (84) to *Pammachius and Oceanus* (circa 399-400 A.D.); ***The Nicene and Post-Nicene Fathers*** (Volume VI) *Letters and Select Works* (Second Series) Translated by W.H. Fremantle, Published originally by (T&T Clark in Edinburgh) cited version by WM. B. Eerdmans Publishing Company, Grand Rapids, Michigan, Reprinted, March 1989, pp. 175-176; It must be *highly-noted* that Saint Jerome (was fluent in Hebrew, Greek, and Latin) and had in his very possession (mid-late to 4th & early 5th centuries) texts (manuscripts) that were "not" extant like they are now; in addition, the Johannes Gutenberg (1393–1406 – 3rd February 1468 † A.D.) Bible (Vulgate: 1454 A.D.) includes the text (*Comma Johanneum*: 1 John 5:7) as well, in Latin, of which is contained in the 1592 edition of the Latin-Vulgate (The Official Bible of the Roman Catholic Church) still to this day! ***Aelius Donatus*** (4th-mid-century) was a Roman Grammarian & (Rhetoric) that taught Saint Jerome, etc., Greek and Latin grammar and punctuation.

[127] Apocalypse 22:19.

S. THEOPHILUS ANTIOCHENUS.

Saint Theophilus (Greek: *Θεόφιλος ὁ Ἀντιοχεύς*; he died circa 183-185 † A.D.) he was Patriarch of Antioch; in his *Discourse to Autolycus*[128] (a pagan) it appears that in his writings[129] he is the first to give us the word "Trinity"[130]:

"In like manner also the three days which were before the luminaries, are types of the Trinity, of God, and His Word, and His wisdom. And the fourth is the type of man, who needs light, that so there may be God, the Word, wisdom, man."[131]

---

[128] ***The Fathers of the Church*** *A New Translation* (Volume 100) by Saint Jerome *On Illustrious Men,* Translated by Thomas P. Halton, Published by the Catholic University Press of America, Washington, D.C., (1999), p. 48; Cf. De viris illustr., c. 25: *breves elegantesque tractus ad aedificationem ecclesiae pertinentes*—(translation mine): *short and elegant tracts relating to the building of the church; See lastly:* ***Patrology*** *The Lives and Works of the Fathers of the Church* by Otto Bardenhewer translated by Thomas J. Mann, Pubisled by B. Herder Books in Saint Louis, Mo, 1908, p. 67.

[129] ***Patrologia Graeca*** ***[Patrologiae Cursus Completus, Series Graeca, edited by*** **Abbé J.P. Migne** ***in 161 Volumes from 1857–1866]*** Vol. 6, pp. 1023-1168; the writings of Saint Theophilus are *extant* (*still existing*) in the citations of *Eusebius of Caesarea* (who was suppressed "and struck out of" the Roman-Martyrology by Pope Gregory XIII) cf. ***A Dictionary of Christian Biography and Literature*** edited by Henry Wace & William C. Piercy, Published by John Murray, London (1911), p. 334; reprinted by Hendrickson Publishers Peabody, Massachusetts (1994), p. 334; and by Saint Jerome who himself gives us these precious writings. *Eusebius of Caesarea* makes mention of Theophilus in his *Ecclesiastical History* in Book IV (4), Chapter XXIV (24).

[130] ***Manual of Patrology*** by F. Cayré, Translated (from French) by H. Howitt, First Volume (First and Second Volumes) Published by Society of St. John The Evangelist, Desclée & Co., Paris France, 1927, p. 134.

[131] ***The Ante-Nicene Fathers*** (Volume II) translated by Alexander Roberts & James Donaldson, Published originally by (T&T Clark in Edinburgh) cited version by

Athenagoras of Athens (Greek: *Ἀθηναγόρας ὁ Ἀθηναῖος*; born 133 – 190 † A.D.) writing in the 2nd century proceeds and instructs (177-178 A.D.)[132] that:

"Who then would not be amazed hearing those called atheists who call God Father and Son and Holy Spirit, proclaiming their power in unity and in rank their diversity?"[133]

Tertullian (Latin: *Quintus Septimius Florens Tertullianus*; 150-160 – 240 A.D.) who became a heretic (Montanism)[134] later in life; declares in (208 AD) thc recorded account (Against the heretic Praxeas):

WM. B. Eerdmans Publishing Company, Grand Rapids, Michigan, Reprinted, March 1994, pp. 100-101.

132 ***Manual of Patrology*** by F. Cayré, Translated (from French) by H. Howitt, First Volume (First and Second Volumes) Published by Society of St. John The Evangelist, Desclée & Co., Paris France, 1927, p. 132.

133 ***The Embassy for the Christians*** (*Chapter 10*), Translated by Joseph Hugh Crehan (Volume 23), Published by the Newman Press in Westminster, Maryland, 1956, p. 40-41; for a variant reading Cf. ***The Ante-Nicene Fathers*** (Volume II) *A Plea for the Christians* (*Chapter 10*), Translated by Alexander Roberts & James Donaldson, Published originally by (T&T Clark in Edinburgh) cited version by WM. B. Eerdmans Publishing Company, Grand Rapids, Michigan, Reprinted, March 1994, p. 133.

134 Saint Jerome mentions the heresies (errors) of Tertullian in his work: ***The Fathers of the Church*** *A New Translation* (Volume 100) by Saint Jerome *On Illustrious Men* (Chapter 53=LIII, section IV=4), Translated by Thomas P. Halton, Published by the Catholic University Press of America, Washington, D.C., (1999), pp. 74-75.

"Bear always in mind that this is the rule of faith which I profess; by it I testify that the Father, and the Son, and the Spirit are inseparable from each other, and so will you know in what sense this is said. Now, observe, my assertion is that the Father is one, and the Son one, and the Spirit one, and that They are distinct from Each Other. This statement is taken in a wrong sense by every uneducated as well as every perversely disposed person, as if it predicated a diversity, in such a sense as to imply a separation among the Father, and the Son, and the Spirit. I am, moreover, obliged to say this, when (extolling the Monarchy at the expense of the Economy) they contend for the identity of the Father and Son and Spirit, that it is not by way of diversity that the Son differs from the Father, but by distribution: it is not by division that He is different, but by distinction; because the Father is not the same as the Son, since they differ one from the other in the mode of their being. For the Father is the entire substance, but the Son is a derivation and portion of the whole, as He Himself acknowledges: 'My Father is greater than I' (John 14:2). In the Psalm His inferiority is described as being 'a little lower than the angels' [Psalm 8:6; Hebrews 2:7] Thus the Father is distinct from the Son, being greater than the Son, inasmuch as He who begets is one, and He who is begotten is another; He, too, who sends is one, and He who is sent is another; and He, again, who makes is one, and He through whom the thing is made is another. Happily the Lord Himself employs this expression of the person of the Paraclete, so as to signify not a division or severance, but a disposition (of mutual relations in the Godhead); for He says, 'I will pray the Father, and He shall send you another Comforter...even the Spirit of truth,' (John 14:16), thus making the Paraclete distinct from Himself, even as we say that the Son is also distinct from the Father; so that He showed a third degree in the Paraclete, as we believe the second degree is in the Son, by reason of the order observed in the Economy. Besides, does not the very fact that they have the distinct names of Father and Son amount to a declaration that they are distinct in personality? For, of course, all things will be what their names represent them to be; and what they are and ever will be, that will they be called; and the distinction indicated by the names does not at all admit of any confusion, because there is none in the things which they designate. 'Yes is yes, and no is no; for what is more than these, comes of evil' (Matthew 5:37)."[135]

Saint Cyprian[136] of Carthage (Latin: *Thascius Caecilius Cyprianus*; 210 to 14th September 258 † A.D.) explicitly writes in (251 A.D.):

[135] Against Praxeas (Greek: ***Πραξέας***) a late (2nd to 3rd century) heretic (like later Tertullian) that died outside the Catholic Church; in Chapter 12 (XII) Tertullian writes against Praxeas [not to be confused with Praxeus] the following account; Cf. ***The Ante-Nicene Fathers*** (Volume III) *Against Praxeas* (*Chapter 12=XII*), Translated by Dr. Holmes, Published originally by (T&T Clark in Edinburgh) cited version by WM. B. Eerdmans Publishing Company, Grand Rapids, Michigan, Reprinted, June 1993, pp. 603-604; Cf. ***The Faith of the Early Fathers*** (Volume 1) Selected and Translated by W.A. Jurgens, Published by The Liturgical Press, Collegeville, Minnesota, 1970, p. 156, Article # 378.

[136] According (and rightfully so) did Saint Augustine of Hippo diligently uphold that Saint Cyprian of Carthage died as a Saint of the Most Holy Roman Church; Cf. ***Nicene And Post-Nicene Fathers*** (Volume IV) *On Baptism, Against the Donatists* (Chapter 5) Translated J.R. King, Published originally by (T&T Clark in Edinburgh) cited version by WM. B. Eerdmans Publishing Company, Grand Rapids, Michigan, Reprinted, May 1989, p. 438; Lastly see (for a variant reading): (I/21) Part I, Volume 21, ***The Donatist Controversy I*** (Book III), *Cyprian's correspondence with Jubaianus*, Translated by Maureen Tilley and Boniface Ramsey, Published by New City Press, Hyde Park, New York, p. 445.

"The spouse of Christ cannot be adulterous; she is uncorrupted and pure. She knows one home; she guards with chaste modesty the sanctity of one couch. She keeps us for God. She appoints the sons whom she has born for the kingdom. Whoever is separated from the Church and is joined to an adulteress, is separated from the promises of the Church; nor can he who forsakes the Church of Christ attain to the rewards of Christ. He is a stranger; he is profane; he is an enemy. He can no longer have God for his Father, who has not the Church for his mother. If any one could escape who was outside the Ark of Noah, then he also may escape who shall be outside of the Church. The Lord warns, saying, 'He who is not with me is against me, and he who gathers not with me scatters' (Matthew 12:30). He who breaks the peace and the concord of Christ, does so in opposition to Christ; he who gathers elsewhere than in the Church, scatters the Church of Christ. The Lord says, 'I and the Father are one' (John 10:30); and again it is written of the Father, and of the Son, and of the Holy Spirit, 'And these three are one' (1 John 5:7). And does any one believe that this unity which thus comes from the divine strength and coheres in celestial sacraments, can be divided in the Church, and can be separated by the parting asunder of opposing wills? He who does not hold this unity does not hold God's law, does not hold the faith of the Father and the Son, does not hold life and salvation."[137]

---

[137] ***The Ante-Nicene Fathers*** (Volume V) *The Treatises of Cyprian* (I=1; Article # VI=6), Translated by Alexander Roberts & James Donaldson, Published originally by (T&T Clark in Edinburgh) cited version by WM. B. Eerdmans Publishing

Saint Cyprian of Carthage continues (To J[I]ubaianus[138], Concerning The Baptism of Heretics) with:

"And so, if someone could be baptized amongst heretics, he could doubtless also receive forgiveness [remission] of sins; and if he received forgiveness [remission] of sins, he was sanctified. If he was sanctified, then he became a temple of God. But of what God, I ask? The Creator? Not possible, seeing that he does not believe in Him. Christ, then? But he cannot become His temple either, for he denies that Christ is God. Or the Holy Spirit [Ghost]? As these three are one[139], how can the Holy Ghost look with favor upon him when he is an enemy either of the Son or of the Father?"[140]

Company, Grand Rapids, Michigan, Reprinted, February 1990, p. 423; Cf. (for a variant reading): ***Ancient Christian Writers*** (Number 25), *St. Cyprian, The Lapsed, and the Unity of the Catholic Church* Translated by Maurice Bévenot, Published by the Newman Press, New York, N.Y., Mahwah, N.J., 1956, pp. 48-49.

[138] ***Saint Cyprian*** writes: "beloved brother" indicating his love for J[I]ubaianus.

[139] 1 John 5:7; however, the Author of this text (Graeme W. Clarke) puts 1 John 5:8 (not verse 7); another note, the Early Church Fathers never used the word "forgive or forgiveness" but they used the word Remission or Remit sin(s) in their respect texts (such as Greek or Latin).

[140] Cf. (for a variant reading): ***Ancient Christian Writers*** (Number 47), *St. Cyprian,* Volume IV (Letter 73), Translated by Graeme W. Clarke, Published by the Newman Press, New York, N.Y., Mahwah, N.J., 1989, p. 60 – see notes for this; See also: ***The Ante-Nicene Fathers*** (Volume V) *The Epistles of Cyprian* (LXXII=72), Translated by Alexander Roberts & James Donaldson, Published originally by (T&T Clark in Edinburgh) cited version by WM. B. Eerdmans Publishing Company, Grand Rapids, Michigan, Reprinted, February 1990, p. 382; Lastly: what is the confusion between these two letters (currently) is beyond me; (Letter 73) ***Ancient Christian Writers*** is cited; and in the ***Ante-Nicene Fathers*** (Letter 72) is cited; there may be a discrepancy among these text(s) in question.

Saint Cyprian writes:

"The Bride of Christ (2 Corinthians 11:2; Ephesians 5:23-32) cannot be defiled. She is inviolate and chaste. She knows but one home, and with a chaste modesty she guards the sanctity of one bedchamber. It is she that keeps us for God, she that seals for the kingdom the sons whom she bore. Whoever is separated from the Church and is joined to an adulteress is separated from the promises of the Church; nor will he that forsakes the Church of Christ attain to the rewards of Christ. He is an alien, a worldling, and an enemy. He cannot have God for his Father who does not have the Church for his Mother. If anyone outside the ark of Noah (1 Peter 3:20) was able to escape, then perhaps someone outside the pale of the Church may escape. ... The Lord says, 'The Father and I are one (John 10:30);' and again, it is written of the Father, Son, and Holy Spirit, 'And the three are one (1 John 5:7).' Does anyone believe that in the Church this unity which proceeds from the divine stability and which is welded together after the heavenly patterns, can be divided, and can be separated by the parting asunder of opposing wills? Whoever holds not fast to this unity holds not to the law of God; neither does he keep faith with the Father and the Son, nor does he have life and salvation."[141]

---

[141] ***The Faith of the Early Fathers***, Selected and Translated by W.A. Jurgens, (Volume I), Published by Liturgical Press, Collegeville, Minnesota, 1970, Article # 557, p. 221; Cf. for a (variant) reading: ***The Fathers of the Church*** *A New Translation Saint Cyprian Treatises* Translated by Roy J. DeFarrari, Published by The Catholic University of America Press, Washington, D.C., 1958, pp100-101; Lastly for a variant reading Cf. ***Ancient Christian Writers*** (Number 25) The Lapsed and

We must keep in mind that the Church (sadly and always) till the end (consummation)[142] has endured smear-campaigns, forgeries, and interpolations down to the present from the enemies (Jews & Heretics) of the Church. Therefore, it is not surprising that the Jews (those deny that Christ is True God and true man) relish (with evil intent) in their (wishes) to destroy (which it *appears*) they have done to the True Church (Catholic); however, nothing is further from the truth—God is in control and His Church (Catholic) currently the Catholic Church is eclipsed[143] as of now. Arians (heretics) and the like have done nothing but corrupt (like the Jews) the Sacred-Scriptures, and to falsify their hidden-agenda—to destroy the Catholic Church. Therefore, it is evident that the Jews and Arians (heretics) are denying The Word of God[144] to countless billions of people(s) by their forgeries and lies. The Council of Nice (Nicene/Nicaea) was held in 325 A.D. and the distortions (about) this Council by the Jews and the Arians (from the time of Christ, and henceforth) are more than grave—*but evil in and of itself.*

Furthermore, it must be admitted that the Early Church (Catholic) under the helm of Saint Peter the Apostle (and his valid *and* licit successors)[145] was destined to Greatness in Her Saints, etc. However, the likes of Cerinthus (Greek: Κήρινθος: born *circa* 49?-to *died* 101? A.D.), Marcion (Bishop of Sinope in Pontus, born *circa* 85-110?—

---

the Unity of the Catholic Church, *St. Cyprian,* Translated by Maurice Bévenot, Published by the Newman Press, New York, N.Y., Mahwah, N.J., 1956, pp. 48-49.

[142] Matthew 28:20.

[143] Ecclesiasticus 17:30; The True Church (Catholic) still exists but is "eclipsed" (obscured) now by the Jews and the Heretics that run (supposedly) the Catholic Church in Rome; however, there is no need to fear for Christ is the Salvation of our Souls. (Latin): *A Cruce Salus—Salvation comes from the Cross.*

[144] John 1:1; Christ (God) is the One and Only True Messiah.

[145] See: ***Papal Vacancy*** (2023) by William DeTucci.

died 160 A.D.), Valentinus (born *circa* 100–*died* 180 A.D.), and Noëtus (230 A.D.) little is known about Noëtus except that he was a priest (of Asia minor) that was kicked-out of the priesthood for his heretical ideas and thoughts, but that did not stop there, the future of the Church (Catholic) undeniably One, Holy, Catholic, and Apostolic would fight off the enemies of the Church and be victorious in Christ (God) The Founder—*until the consummation*[146] *of the World.* In addition, what did all of the above mentioned heretics have in common—they were all Gnostics[147] (Jews & Pseudo-Christians) and taught (falsely) their doctrines and praxis (practice) to men driving many from the Bark[148] of Saint Peter, The Most Holy Roman Catholic Church—*outside of which there is neither Salvation nor the Remission of Sins.*[149]

---

[146] Matthew 28:20.

[147] The Gnostics (Gnosis=Secret knowledge) took inspiration from the Bible and from the Philosopher *Plato (Greek: Πλάτων* 427 – 348: a.C.n.) *ante Christum natum*=before Christ was born. The original Gnostics whether (Heretics) Jews or Greeks (but flourished into smaller pseudo-Christian sects) they thought they were the "enlightened ones" that "truly" followed God; men are most shocked when they "die" because they were not in the True Catholic Church of Christ (God) but "followed" their own doctrines (or followers of another sect) by many of their (so-called) teachers, etc…many-self-appointed teacher(s) that raped and robbed or in a mysterious way claimed Holy Orders by way of being ordained to the (diaconate or the priesthood; and some that sadly became bishops) they will "all" go down to eternal–flames of hell for eternity *unless they are joined to the Catholic* (Church) *faith and praxis prior to their death* (The Papal Bull ***Cantate Domino***, issued on 4th February 1442 by His Holiness of Blessed Memory Pope Eugene IV † A.D.).

[148] Luke 5:1-10; 1 Peter 3:20-21.

[149] Pope Boniface VIII Papal Bull ***Unam Sanctam*** (November 18th 1302 A.D.); Lastly see: ***Denzinger*** (The Sources of Catholic Dogma), Translated by Roy J. Deferrari, from the Thirtieth (30th) Edition, Published by B. Herder Book Co., St. Louis, Mo., and London, W.C., 1957, pp. 186-187, Article(s) # 468-469; Thereby, it is wholly (understandable that this Dogma of Pope Boniface did not animate at the time or was turned into a rule (or of *New*) faith; however, this Doctrine (Dogma) was always (perpetually) true and real from when Christ Rose from the Dead and asked Peter if he loved Him (John 21:15-17)? Truth does not

Saint Gregory of Nazianzus [Nazianzen]—Greek: ***Γρηγόριος ὁ Ναζιανζηνός*** (329?—390? † A.D.), from these citations from the Archbishop of Constantinople it is reckoned concerning 1 John 5:7 in these strong and Holy words (written in circa 385 A.D.):

Domenichino, S. Gregorio Nazianzeno, 1608-10, Cappella di S. Nilo, Grottaferrata

"What about John then, when in his Catholic Epistle he says that there are Three that bear witness, the Spirit and the Water and the Blood [1 John 5:8]? Do you think he is talking nonsense? First, because he has ventured to reckon under one numeral things which are not consubstantial, though you say this ought to be done only in the case of things which are consubstantial. For who would assert that these are consubstantial? Secondly, because he has not been consistent in the way he has happened upon his terms; for after using Three in the masculine gender he adds three words which are neuter, contrary to the definitions and laws which you and your grammarians have laid down. For what is the difference [1 John 5:7] between putting a masculine Three first, and then adding One and One and One in the neuter, or after a masculine One and One and One to use the Three not in the masculine but in the neuter, which you yourself disclaim in the case of Deity?"[150]

---

change—people do change—*but not the Catholic (Church) Faith and* God=Christ (Malachias 3:6). Amen.

[150] ***The Fifth Theological Oration*** (On the Holy Spirit) by Saint Gregory of Nazianzus-(Nazianzen) Chapter XIX (19); ***The Nicene and Post-Nicene Fathers*** (Volume VII) S. Cyril of Jerusalem & S. Gregory of Nazianzen (Second Series) Translated by W.H. Fremantle, Published originally by (T&T Clark in Edinburgh)

Saint Jerome in his Prologue (388-390 A.D.) annunciates the following writing (Prologue) ***to Eustochium***[151] (Saint):

"Si ab interpretibus fideliter in latinum eloquium verterentur nec ambiguitatem legentibus facerent nec trinitatis unitate in prima joannis epistola positum legimus, in qua etiam, trium tantummodo vocabula hoc est aquae, sanguinis et spiritus in ipsa sua editione ponentes et patris verbique ac spiritus testimoninum omittentes, in quo maxime et fides catholica roboratur, et Patris et Filii et Spirtus Sancti una divinitatis substantia comprobatur.—(Translation mine): If they faithfully translated into the Latin language and create no ambiguity for readers and the variety and create no ambiguity for readers and the variety of words does not contradict itself. In that place, particularly where we read about the unity of the Trinity which is placed in the First Epistle of John, in which also the names of three, i.e. of water, of blood, and of spirit, do they place in their edition and omitting the testimony of the Father, and the Word, and the Spirit, in which the Catholic faith is especially confirmed and the single substance of the Father, the Son, and the Holy Spirit is confirmed."[152]

---

cited version by WM. B. Eerdmans Publishing Company, Grand Rapids, Michigan, Reprinted, March 1989, pp. 323-324.

[151] Saint Eustochium (She) was ***born*** 368 in Rome, ***Died*** Jerusalem 419-420 † A.D.

[152] First (in German) Cf., KARDINAL (Cardinal Guglielmo Sirleto) WILHELM SIRLETS (1514-1585 † A.D.) ANNOTATIONEN ZUM NEUEN TESTAMENT: EINE VERTBIDIGUNG DER VULGATA GEGEN VALLA UND ERASMUS (*A Defense of the Vulgate against Valla and Erasmus*) Edited by P. HILDEBRAND H0PFL O. S. B., Published by Freiburg im Breisgau: Berdersche Verlag & St. Louis, Mo., 1908, pp. 65-66; Cf. ***Codex Fuldensis*** (541-546 A.D.): *Novum*

Socrates Scholasticus (Greek: Σωκράτης ὁ Σχολαστικός; *born* circa 380-408?—*died* 450-460? A.D.) he writes in his ecclesiastical history (323-439) the following:

SOCRATES SCHOLASTICUS

"But having been detected in his sacrilegious career, he made his escape thence and sought refuge in Nicomedia, where he implored the protection of the party of Eusebius; who from their hatred to Athanasius, not only received him as a presbyter, but even promised to confer upon him the dignity of the episcopacy, if he would frame an accusation against Athanasius, listening as a pretext for this to whatever stories Ischyras had invented. For he spread a report that he had suffered dreadfully in consequence of an assault; and that Macarius had rushed furiously toward the altar, had overturned the table, and broken a

---

Testamentum Latine Interprete Hieronymo by Ernestus Ranke, Published by MARBURGI & LIPSIAE, SUMTIBUS N. G. ELWERTI BIBLIOPOLAE ACADEMICI, (MDCCCLXVIII) 1868, pp. 399-400; Furthermore, while the citation is not in the "text" (of *Codex Fuldensis*) itself—Jerome's Prologue (388-390 A.D.) certainly is there (in the ***Codex Fuldensis***) prior to edition set forth. It is very true and real how the Heretics (Jews, Gnostics, and many other so-called sects of Perdition tampered with the Holy-Scriptures) in their pristine (original) and manuscript copies, etc…The Catholic Church has fought and has won the battle(s); however, when the time comes the Church will be eclipsed and maligned greatly for the Church Militant will shine out of the eclipsed sun and win the War of wars with Christ (God) as its Head. Moreover, mention must be made that while few versions (as twisted and deranged and heretical as they are) do contain this verse: The Reims (1582) does; The KJV (1610/1769 ed.) does; and the Rheims (1749-1752) does contain the verse: 1 John 5:7. However, many other so-called (old and new) modern "translations" do not contain the verse in question of 1 John 5:7.

mystical cup: he added also that he had burnt the sacred books [The Holy Bible(s)]."[153]

One thing, here, that must be highly noted that: Emperor Diocletian (Latin: *Gaius Aurelius Valerius Diocletianus*; Ancient Greek: *Διοκλητιανός*) had reigned from (284-305 A.D.) which was the ultra-suppression and persecution of the Christians (both East and West) of the Catholic Church at the time. Emperor Diocletian (*born* 22nd December 242-305 A.D.) ordered the burning and destruction of "all" Churches and Holy Book(s), namely, the Holy-Scriptures.

Furthermore, it must be remembered that Emperor Diocletian's reign was the last persecution of Christians (Catholics) in the known-world (303-312 A.D.), and that, it was not until the Protestant-Reformation where countless souls were either converted-over to (*damnation*, Protestantism) or were persecuted and died under the Protestant Reformation (as True Catholics). Whereby, Emperor Diocletian persecuted the Christians (Catholics) with his last, largest, and bloodiest persecution of Christians (Catholics) was met; however, Emperor Constantine[154] (born *Flavius Valerius Constantinus*) gave the

---

[153] ***The Ecclesiastical** (Church) **History*** by Socrates Scholasticus Book I, Chapter XXVII (27); Cf. ***The Nicene and Post-Nicene Fathers*** (Volume II) ***The Ecclesiastical** (Church) **History*** by Socrates Scholasticus (Second Series) Translated by A.C. Zenos, Published originally by (T&T Clark in Edinburgh) cited version by WM. B. Eerdmans Publishing Company, Grand Rapids, Michigan, Reprinted, July 1989, pp. 28-29.

[154] Constantine I (27th February 272 – 22nd May 337 A.D.) was not at this time "baptized" (Cf. CHAPTER 2, HIERONYMI CHRONICON: *A TRANSLATION OF JEROME'S CONTINUATION OF EUSEBIUS' CHRONICLE FROM AD 327 TO 379* [234a]; A TRANSLATION OF JEROME'S CHRONICON WITH HISTORICAL COMMENTARY by (Translated) Malcolm Drew Donalson, Published by Mellen University Press Lewiston/Queenston/Lampeter (UK), Printed in the United States by The Edwin Mellen Press Lewiston, New York USA, 1996,

Christians (Catholics) civil-rights to retain their Christian-beliefs in February (313 A.D.) with *the Edit of Milan* (Latin: *Edictum Mediolanense*).

The utter and complete chaos outside the Catholic Church was incredible; not to mention unrelenting. Emperor Diocletian destroyed Churches, Book(s) Holy, and even killed many Christians (Catholics) in his bloody reign that lasted even after his death in (305 A.D.)! Never has the Church (of God) been without tears, penance, and an onslaught (attack) from the Jews and Heretics.

Frederick Nolan (1784–1864) was an Irish-Anglican-theologian, he comments as thus:

"Let us add to these considerations, these further circumstances; that the pious emperour [emperor] who had employed him to revise the text, had been at considerable pains and expence [expense] to multiply copies of the scripture; and that the edition thus dispersed, as altered by Eusebius, was peculiarly accommodated to the opinions of the Arians who from the reign of Constantine to that of Theodosius,

---

p. 42; and deferred the Sacrament of Baptism only until (May 22nd 337 A.D.) his (near) death by an Arian-heretic (Eusebius of Nicomedia) who was at this time only a priest, however, in (339-341 A.D.) he took on the role of Archbishop of Nicomedia; Ancyra [Ankara: where Constantine I was baptized] near Nicomedia; Cf. Book Ten (10) – 5 or 10:5 (section 5 of Book 10) of *Rufinus of Aquileia, History of the Church*; in addition, see: "Six only there were who suffered themselves to be expelled with Arius, while the other eleven, after taking counsel together, agreed to subscribe with their hands only, but not their hearts. The chief designer of this pretense was Eusebius. Bishop of Nicomedia" (Cf. ***The Fathers of the Church*** - Volume 133 - *Rufinus of Aquileia, History of the Church*, Translated by Philip R. Amidon, Published by The Catholic University of America Press, Washington, D.C., 2016, p. 385). The Catholic Church does not "hail" Constantine I as a Saint of the Church, etc.

held an unlimited sway over the church; and there will arise something more than presumptive proof in favour [favor] of the opinion which I have advanced; that at this period an alteration was made in the sacred text, of which it still retains a melancholy evidence, particularly in the translations made from the edition of Eusebius."[155]

If one pays attention to the above mentioned, it states very clearly that: "…the Arians who from the reign of Constantine to that of Theodosius, *held an unlimited sway over the church…*" Furthermore, it only demonstrates the mayhem and heresy that the Arians were (at this time) capable of through the intercession of Satan[156].

KARDINAL *(Cardinal Guglielmo Sirleto)* ***WILHELM SIRLETS*** (1514-1585 † A.D.) contests and writes in these Holy-words:

"Jerome says[157] that unscrupulous translators have omitted this testimony; this suggests that it was in the Greek codices before[158]; we can therefore conclude that in his time the Greek writers had not yet grasped this position. But, if one were to

---

[155] ***An Inquiry into the Integrity of the Greek Vulgate*** *or Received Text of the New Testament* by Frederick Nolan, Published in London, 1815, pp. 28-29.

[156] Satan is behind the falls, errors (heresies), sins, and chaos of different sects of men and its institutions—*but not that of* God's (Christ) Church—the Catholic Church (Matthew 16:18-19).

[157] ***Codex Fuldensis*** (541-546 A.D.): *Novum Testamentum Latine Interprete Hieronymo* by Ernestus Ranke, Published by MARBURGI & LIPSIAE, SUMTIBUS N. G. ELWERTI BIBLIOPOLAE ACADEMICI, (MDCCCLXVIII) 1868, pp. 399-400

[158] The Jews had their greedy-hands on this most-sacred texts and manuscripts,

object, it is quite improbable that this passage is corrupted, since [Saint] Cyril [of Jerusalem], who lived in Rome 1100 years, before us, never cites it, but only the words: *tres aunt qui testimonium sunt, spiritus, aqua et sanguis* [*There are three that bear witness: spirit, water, and blood.*], that I do not deny that Cyril only cited these words, and I am even sure that [Saint] Gregory of Nazianzus [Nazianzen], who lived before Cyril and had a greater reputation, also quoted these words, as did Pope Leo in his letter to Flavian. But we cannot conclude with absolute certainty that the passage: *There are three who bear witness in heaven*, etc., was unknown to them. It is not only St. Jerome who supports the Johannine [Johanneum] origin of the same, but also Athanasius, Patriarch of Alexandria, who in his writing *De fide* (*On the Faith*) also says: Ignores quia pater Deus unus est et filius unus Deus et spiritus sanctus unus Deus est? Unitum nomen est, quia una est eoram substantia, node et Joannes in epistola sua ait: tres aunt qui testimonium dant in caelo, pater, verbum et spiritus, et unum sunt, non tantum unus est, quia non est eorum una persona (Translation mine)—Do you not know that the Father is one God and the Son is one God and the Spirit is God yet they are three but one God? It is a single name, because their substance is one, as John also says in his epistle [1 John 5:7]: '*There are three who bear witness in heaven, the Father, the Word, and the Spirit, and they are one,*' not only one, because they are not one[159] person."[160]

---

[159] Therefore, there are three (3) Divine Persons – yet ONE True Eternal God.

[160] ***KARDINAL*** *(Cardinal Guglielmo Sirleto)* ***WILHELM SIRLETS*** (1514-1585 † A.D.) ANNOTATIONEN ZUM NEUEN TESTAMENT: EINE VERTBIDIGUNG DER VULGATA GEGEN VALLA UND ERASMUS (*A Defense of the Vulgate against Valla and Erasmus*) Edited by P. HILDEBRAND H0PFL O. S. B., Published by Freiburg im Breisgau: Berdersche Verlag & St. Louis, Mo., 1908, p. 66.

Bishop Victor[161] Vitensis (*born circa* 430 A.D.–?) writes in his famous work called, *Historia persecutionis Africanae Provinciae*:

"Et ut adhuc luce clarius unius diuinitatis esse cum patre et filio spiritum sanctum doceamus, lohannis euangelisetae testimonium conprobatur. Ait namque; tres sunt qui testimonium perhibent in caelo, pater, uerbum et spiritus sanctus, et hi tres unum sunt Numquid ait: 'tres in differentiae qualitate seiuneti aut quibeslibet diuersitatam gradibus longo separationis interuallo diuisi (1 John 5:7).' (Translation mine)—And in order that we may still more clearly teach the Holy Spirit that there is one Godhead with the Father and the Son, the testimony of John the Evangelist is confirmed. For he said: 'There are three who give witness in heaven, the Father, the Word, and the Holy Spirit, and these three are one. (1 John 5:7).' "[162]

---

[161] Also known as *Victor Vita*, Bishop of Vita in the African province of Byzacena; sadly, this was not a general persecution of Christianity (Arian-heretics) but especially against the Catholic Church. The barbarian Vandals at the time were semi-Arians (at the time) which later they converted to Catholicism.

[162] ***VICTORIS VITENSIS*** *HISTORIA PERSECUTIONIS AFRICANAE PROVINCIAE SUB GEISERICO ET HUNIRICO REGIBUS WANDALORUM*, RECENSUIT (Edited and Reviewed) by CAROLUS HALM, Published in BEROLINI (Berlin) APUD (at) WEIDMANNOS, MDCCCLXXVIIII=1878, pp. 33-34; ***Uictoris Uitensis*** (***Victoris Vitensis***), *Historia persecutionis Africanae Provinciae, LIBER FIDEI CATHOLICAE,* (Liber II=Book II, # Article 82); Cf. Uictoris Uitensis, *Historia persecutionis Africanae Provinciae,* (Liber II=Book II, Article 82, LIBER FIDEI CATHOLICAE, Published by (CSEL) *Corpus Scriptorum Ecclesiasticorum* Editum Consilio Et Impensis, Academiae Litterarum Caesareae Vindobonensis, Vol. VII=7, **Victoris Episcopi Vitensis** *Historia Persecutionis Africanae Provinciae (A History of the African Province Persecution),* Ex Recensione Michaelis Petschenio, Vindobonae Apud C. Geroldi Filium

Likewise, the *Codex* [*Fuldensis*][163] *Freisingensis* (dated to the 5th or 6th century) has the Johanneum Comma (1 John 5:7) in it.

Saint Fulgentius[164] of Ruspe (Northern Africa: *born* 467/468? – *died* 1st January 532/533? A.D.) who is considered the Greatest Theologian after Saint Augustine, plainly and clearly writes:

"And the Son is eternal and without beginning, because the Son, born from the nature of the Father, has always existed. And the Holy Spirit is eternal and without beginning, because the Holy Spirit proceeds from the nature of the Father and the Son. So, therefore, rightly do we believe and say that the three are one God [1 John 5:7], because there is a single eternity, a single immensity, a single divinity by nature of three persons."[165]

Bibliopolam Academiae, MDCCCLXXXI=1881, p. 60; Cf. ***Patrologia Latina*** (Volume LVIII=58), by J.P. Mingé, 1862, p. 227C, or Column 227C, LIBER TERTIUS (The Third Book). *PROFESSIO FIDEI CATHOLICORUM EPISCOPORUM HUNERICO REGI OBLATA*—(Translation mine): *PROFESSION OF THE FAITH OF THE CATHOLIC BISHOPS OFFERED TO THE HUNRICIAN KING.*

163 ***Patrologia Latina*** (Volume XXVIIII=29), by J.P. Mingé, 1846, (or columns) p. 827-831; see also: *Beware* of the Different Codex's [A.D. 546] to the *Fuldensis* as they are not all the same and differ greatly.

164 Cf. footnote # 3 on p. 191 of ***A Manual of Patrology*** by F. Cayre, Translated by H. Howitt (Second Volume II) Third and Fourth Works, Published by Society of St. John The Evangelist, by Desclée & Co (1930)., Paris, Tournai, Rome, 1940 (First Printed in Belgium), p. 191.

165 ***The Fathers of the Church: A New Translation, Fulgentius Selected Works*** (Volume 95; *Letter To Peter On the Faith*: Article # 4) Translated by Robert B.

And Saint Fulgentius repeats again:

"And when you hear of the Trinity, Father, Son, and Holy Spirit, recognize the three persons [1 John 5:7] of that one most high divinity. For there are three persons, the Father and the Son and the Holy Spirit; thus, it is called the Trinity but there is one substance of the Father and the Son and the Holy Spirit. Therefore, the Trinity itself is truly proclaimed as one God by the faithful."[166]

And again, Saint Fulgentius is cited:

"If you hear anyone speaking of the three persons [1 John 5:7] of the Father and the Son and the Holy Spirit in such a way that they want to assert three natures of these three persons, understand without a doubt that he is an Arian heretic. It is true that the Sabellians believe in the one nature of the Father and the Son and the Holy Spirit; but it is false because they do not believe in the three persons. It is also true that Arians say that there are three persons [1 John 5:7] of the Father and the Son and the Holy Spirit; but it is false because they strive to persuade us that there are three natures of these three persons. Therefore, perversely do the Arians divide the nature of the Trinity and Sabellians confuse the persons; since the nature of the Father and the

---

Eno, Published by The Catholic University of America Press, Washington, D.C., (1997), pp. 62-63.

[166] Ibid., pp. 367-368, (Letter VIII=8 to Donatus, Articles # 3).

Son and the Holy Spirit is one in such a way that there is one person of the Father, another of the Son, and a third of the Holy Spirit."[167]

Saint Fulgentius clearly writes:

"Let this perversity be far from the faithful, nor may God permit anyone redeemed by the blood of his only-begotten Son to be thus profaned by the death-dealing sense of faithlessness. It is a matter of great impiety if anyone either wishes to proclaim one person because of one nature in the Father and the Son and the Holy Spirit or, because of the three persons [1 John 5:7], asserts three natures as well. Inasmuch as he who asserts that there is one person of the Father and the Son and the Holy Spirit is caught in the snare of the Sabellian error; on the other hand, the one who confirms that there are three natures of the Father and the Son and the Holy Spirit is entangled in the cords of Arian faithlessness. And although the assertion of each form of infidelity seems different, the condemnation for each type of impiety is one. Because of the unity of nature, what is proper to the persons is impiously confused; no less impiously is unity of nature broken up because of the properties of the persons."[168]

---

[167] Ibid., p. 379, (Letter VIII=8 to Donatus, Articles # 3).
[168] Ibid., p. 429, (*Letter to THE BOOK OF ST. FULGENTIUS THE BISHOP TO SCARILA CONCERNING THE INCARNATION OF THE SON OF GOD AND THE AUTHOR OF VILE ANIMALS*. Article #6).

Our Saint, Fulgentius, confreres and teaches as follows:

"Therefore, in all of these we find the word both in the singular and in the plural; the plural because the very quality of the nature shows that all creatures are separable; but singular because in order that there be one soul, one spirit, one virgin, one Church, one light, this that one Trinity has brought about by its grace; this in nature as well as in the persons is inseparable in such a way that whatever there is said about the one as well as about the three persons [1 John 5:7] in the singular is not said in the plural. Therefore, the persons of the Father and the Son and the Holy Spirit cannot be separated, for whom one name by nature is so fitting that there cannot be a plural in the three persons; with the exception of this by which they are called persons, there can be no other name in the Father and the Son and the Holy Spirit which is not given in the singular only. But scarcely could the inadequacy of human speech find this one so that at least it would say that there are three persons; so that if even this were not said, that there is a Trinity would not be believed and from that complete silence, a danger to faith would be born."[169]

---

[169] Ibid., p. 506, (***LETTER 14***. *THE LETTER OF FULGENTIUS TO FERRANDUS*, Article # 7).

Saint Fulgentius cites Saint Augustine:

" 'Likewise, further on, the same Saint Augustine speaks as follows: 'From the many modes of expression in the divine books, we have already shown that what is said about each one in this Trinity is likewise said about all of them, on account of the inseparable activity of the one and the same substance.'[170] In the fifteenth book of *On the Trinity* when, concerning this image that is within us, he wished to put forward some lines for the understanding of the Trinity, among other things he says, 'On the contrary, the inseparability in that highest Trinity, which incomparably surpasses all things, is so great that although a trinity of men cannot be called one man, yet that Trinity is called and is one God, nor is that Trinity in one God but it is the one God. Nor again, as this image, which the man is who has these three, is one person, so is that Trinity ... but there are three persons [1 John 5:7], the Father of the Son, the Son of the Father, and the Spirit of both the Father and the Son.'[171] In the same fashion, after a bit, he says, 'Yet we do not find that, as in this image of the Trinity, these three are not the one man but belong to the one man, so in the highest Trinity itself, whose image this is, are those three of one God, but they are the one God, and there are three persons, not one.'[172] "[173]

---

[170] ***CCL*** (***Corpus Christianorum Series Latina***. Turnhout: Brepols, 1953-) Volume 50, p.64.; FOTC 45·37; ***The Fathers of the Church—FOTC*** (Volume 45) *A New Translation* (*Saint Augustine The Trinity*) Translated by Stephen Mckenna, Published by Catholic University of America Press, Washington, D.C., (Book I, Chapter 12, Article # 25), 1963, p. 37.

[171] ***CCL*** (***Corpus Christianorum Series Latina***. Turnhout: Brepols, 1953-) Volume 50A, pp. 520-21; Cf. ***The Fathers of the Church—FOTC*** (Volume 45) *A New Translation* (*Saint Augustine The Trinity*) Translated by Stephen Mckenna, Published by Catholic University of America Press, Washington, D.C., (Book XV=15, Chapter 23, Article # 43), 1963, p. 509.

[172] ***The Fathers of the Church—FOTC*** (Volume 45) *A New Translation* (*Saint Augustine The Trinity*) Translated by Stephen Mckenna, Published by

Saint Fulgentius boldly and correctly declares on (1 John5:7):

"[**14.**] I have no doubt that these words of the blessed Augustine which we have cited from the first and last book of *On the Trinity* are completely sufficient; especially with your intelligence and interest with which you very frequently and with understanding read his words, so that you are able to find in them many similar things which show the inseparability of the Holy Trinity, not only in nature but also in the persons. Therefore, these three persons [1 John 5:7] are spoken of one by one that they may be known, not that they may be separated, in whom there is no separation, just as there can be no confusion in them. Nor must those three persons [1 John 5:7] because they cannot be confused on that account be considered as separable since they are altogether inseparable both in what they are and in what they do. And let no one dare to assert that those three persons are separable since he is able to find none either existing or acting before another, none after another, none without another. Where just as by nature there can be no separability of action, there by nature remains an incomparable unity of will."[174]

Catholic University of America Press, Washington, D.C., (Book XV=15, Chapter 23, Article # 43), 1963, p. 510.

[173] Letter 14. *THE LETTER OF FULGENTIUS TO FERRANDUS,* Article # 13; Cf. ***The Fathers of the Church: A New Translation, Fulgentius Selected Works*** (Volume 95) Translated by Robert B. Eno, Published by The Catholic University of America Press, Washington, D.C., (1997), p. 515.

[174] ***Letter 14***. *THE LETTER OF FULGENTIUS TO FERRANDUS,* Article # 14; Cf. ***The Fathers of the Church: A New Translation, Fulgentius Selected Works*** (Volume 95) Translated by Robert B. Eno, Published by The Catholic University of America Press, Washington, D.C., (1997), p. 516.

Saint Fulgentius writing in (510 A.D. circa) defending the Holy Dogma of the Blessed Trinity, writes:

"See, in short you have it that the Father is one, the Son another, and the Holy Spirit another; in Person, each is other, but in nature they are not other. In this regard He says: 'The Father and I, we are one (John 10:30).' He teaches us that *one* refers to Their nature, and *we are* to Their persons. In like manner it is said: 'There are three who bear witness in heaven, the Father, the Word, and the Spirit; and these three are one (1 John 5:7).' Let Sabellius hear *we are*, let him hear *three*; and let him believe that there are three Persons. Let him not blaspheme in his sacrilegious heart by saying that the Father is the same in Himself as the Son is the same in Himself and as the Holy Spirit is the same in Himself, as if in some way He could beget Himself, or in some way proceed from Himself. Even in created natures it is never able to be found that something is able to beget itself (1 John 5:7). Let also Arius hear *one*; and let him not say that the Son is of a different nature, if one cannot be said of that, the nature of which is different."[175]

---

[175] *To Trasamund*, ***The Trinity, or De Trinitate ad Felicem***—(Translation mine)—*On the Trinity to Felix*; Cf. ***Patrologia Latina*** by Abbé Minge, Vol. 65, pp. 497-508; Cf. ***Corpus Christianorum***—(Translation mine)—(*The Body or Christians*), Vol. 91 A, (1968), pp. 633-646. See also: ***The Faith of the Early Fathers*** (Volume 3) Selected and Translated by W.A. Jurgens, Published by The Liturgical Press, Collegeville, Minnesota, 1979, p. 291, Article # 2251.

Magnus Aurelius Cassiodorus Senator—simply known as *Cassiodorus* (477-570 † A.D.) he was a Roman-Statesman and in 540[176] A.D. he left the world to retire as a Monastic at the age of sixty (60) years old. Cassiodorus[177] states on the (Holy-Bible) the following:

"οτι τρεις εισιν οι μαρτυρουντες εν τω ουρανω ο πατηρ ο λογος και το αγιον πνευμα και ουτοι οι τρεις εν εισιν—For there are three that bear record in heaven, the Father, the (Son) Word[178], and the Holy Ghost: and these three are one."[179]

The damnable[180] and heretical-Jews have done nothing but to "try" in their (*vain*) attempt to overthrow the Kingdom of Christ[181] (God) with

---

[176] **Manual of Patrology** by F. Cayré, Translated (from French) by H. Howitt, Volume II, Published by Society of St. John The Evangelist, Desclée & Co., Paris France, 1930, p. 223.

[177] Cassiodorus knew both Greek & Latin.

[178] ***Epistola S. Joannis Ad Parthos*** (*Epistle of St. John to Parthos*), *Complexiones in Epistola Apost.*—(*Complexions in the Epistle Apostle.*) by Cassiodorus (Cassiodori) # 11-12; Cf. ***Patrologia Latina*** by Abbé Minge, Vol. 70, pp. 1373-1374 A-D (footnotes as well); See also: ***The Anchor Bible****: The Epistles of John* (Volume 30) by Raymond E. Brown, Published by Doubleday & Company in Garden City, New York, 1982, p. 775., (Cf. Appendix IV: The Johannine Comma, Footnote # 1). *The heretic* (Raymond E. Brown) would cite Cassiodorus (1 John 5:7) as occasionally stating: " 'Son' is read for 'Word' in the Comma (e.g., Cassiodorus).' "

[179] 1 John 5:7; the Greek text reads…

[180] Matthew 28:11-15.

[181] The One and Only True *Messias—Messiah* is Christ (The God-man).

their denial of 1 John 5:7. This verse (or comma)[182] is a bullet to their eyes. The utter denial of this verse of Sacred-Scripture is incredible not to mention that the Jews[183] will suffer the greatest of pains in hell for *their denial* (and forgery) of the Blessed Trinity in this passage: 1 John 5:7.

Why the emphasis on the Jews? The Jews reject Christ[184] (God), and, they try (as it appears), to make light or fun of the fact that Christ did not rise (by His own power) from the Dead? This is absolute rubbish and *extremely* far from the Truth! Christ rose from the Dead by His own power! When we look at the Holy-Scriptures one (it appears) has a sense that not all men will be saved but very few will find eternal-life. Am I (your author) trying to pull a fast one on you? Think again! Did not Noah's Ark save only eight (8) people—is this made up or the truth? Of course, only eight (8) souls[185] were saved by water (a reference to the Holy Sacrament of Baptism: John 3:5). The *scarcity* of souls that will be saved[186] at the Apocalypse (*end of the world)* will be great indeed; even though God has called all men to penance (1 Timothy 2:4) in each and every era of History, the number of *the elect* (will be relatively small) in comparison to the damned.

---

[182] *Comma* is a short phrase or sentence.
[183] Apocalypse 2:9, 3:9.
[184] Christ (God) is the *Messias*—(*Messiah*) that came to save (John 3:16) not to destroy souls (like Satan does); John 1:41; John 4:25.
[185] 1 Peter 3:20.
[186] Matthew 7:14, 9:37, 15:34, 20:16, 22:14

Saint Isidore of Seville was Archbishop of Seville (Latin: *Isidorus Hispalensis*; was *born* in Spain in *Cartagena* in 560 – he *died* in Seville on 4th April 636 † A.D.) he thus teaches on 1 John 5:7 the following:

"In Epistola Joannis. *Quoniam tres sunt qui testimonium dant in terra , Spiritus, aqua , et Sanguis; et tres unum sunt in Christo Jesu ; et tres sunt, qui testimonium dicunt in cœlo, Pater, Verbum, et Spiritus, et tres unum sunt. In Epistola II.* Quoniam multi fallaces prodierunt in hunc mundum, qui non eonfitentur, Dominum nostrum Jesum in carne venisse, hi sunt fallaces, et antichristi sunt. (Translation mine)—In the Epistle of John. *For there are three who they bear witness on earth, Spirit, water, and Blood; and the three are one in Christ Jesus; and there are three who testify in heaven, the Father, the Son, and the Spirit, and the three are one.* '[187] *In Epistle II.* Because many deceivers have come into this world, who do not believe that our Lord Jesus has come in the flesh, these are deceivers and are antichrists[188] (2 John 1:7)."[189]

---

[187] It may be that the reason for the first statement was rather "mixed" or may be a way of pre-language style for it (appears) odd that the Comma (Johanneum) comes after verse 1 John 5:8?

[188] Anyone (can be) an Antichrist(s) by his thoughts, words, deeds, or even by omitting to do something, and therefore, the Apostle (John) warns us to be very wary and on guard at all times for the enemy does not sleep.

[189] ***Patrologia Latina*** by Abbé Minge, Vol. 83, (1862), p. 1203C, Sancti Isidori, Hispalensus Episcopi, Opera Omina: *Testimonia Divinae Scripturae, Et Patrum—*

While the *Codex Fuldensis* (546 A.D.) does not have the passage in it (1 John 5:7)[190], it does however have Saint Jerome's *Prologue* to the matter at hand which appears odd (strange). Again, the Jews have done nothing but try to make havoc[191] among the Church of God (The Catholic Church). It must be stated here that *The Theological Library of Caesarea Maritima* (Israel), or simply the *Library of Caesarea*, was destroyed by Muslims (Arabs) in 638[192] A.D. in which it included over 30,000 manuscripts[193] (volumes, etc.) of Christian writings. The likes of: (Sts.) Pamphilus (*died* 309 † A.D.), Gregory Nazianzus (329–May 9th 390 † A.D.), Basil the Great (329-379 † A.D.), Jerome (342-September 30th 420 † A.D.) and others came to study there. It is a fact that heretics like Tertullian (155 – 220 A.D.), Origen (185 – 253 A.D.), Arius (250 *or* 256 – 336 A.D.), Priscillian (4th century), Facundus of Hermiane (Hermiana, 6th century), Jacob of Edessa (640 – 5th June 708 A.D.), and many others that either cited: 1 John 5:7, (or) weeded it out of the Holy-Scriptures therefore decimating the verse (phrase) in question: *"And there are three who testify (record) in heaven, the Father, the Son, and the Spirit, and the three are one."*[194]

(Translation mine) *Testimony of the Divine Scriptures, and of the Fathers* (see Appendix XI).

[190] That's: "For there are three that bear record in heaven, the Father, the (Son) Word, and the Holy Ghost: and these three are one (1 John 5:7)."

[191] Cf. the work: ***Epiphanius of Salamis****: DOCTOR OF ICONOCLASM? Deconstruction of a Myth* by Steven Bigham, Published by Orthodox Research Institute, in Rollinsford, NH., (2008), numbering 161 pages. Furthermore, the Jews are responsible for these outlandish (foreign) and heretical-views and ideas against: Saint Epiphanius.

[192] This is the same year that the infidel (Muslims) took over Jerusalem in Israel.

[193] The Volumes (Manuscripts) of these works and the Greek and Latin texts must have been staggering to the Church in the invasion of the Muslim (Arabs). Not to mention that there had to be early copies of the Greek (mostly) and Latin texts of the New Testament that were destroyed by the infidel (Muslims).

[194] 1 John 5:7.

Besides this, it should be further evidence and with a strong-persuasion that (1 John 5:7) is most-authentic and worthy to be placed in: ***The Holy Latin Vulgate Bible of 1592*** (A.D.). Of which is based off of Saint Jerome's Latin Vulgate without question. The Holy-Scriptures (The Bible) of the aforesaid is "Infallible" and without any error (or heresy) of *any* kind(s) whatsoever! The Holy 19th Ecumenical Council of Trent (Session 4) teaches us solemnly that:

"If anyone should not accept as sacred and canonical these entire books and all their parts as they have, by established custom, been read in the Catholic Church, and as contained in the old Latin Vulgate edition, and in conscious judgment should reject the aforesaid traditions: let him be anathema."[195]

Without doubt the True Faith (Catholic) will remain (abide) while the heretics of hell (and unbelief) will scorn the faith of the Apostles Peter and Paul forever and ever amen! Therefore the Sixto-Clementine Vulgate (1592 ed.) remains as the book of Infallibility and Wisdom from Christ (God) Himself.

---

[195] Papal Encyclical (His Holiness of Blessed Memory Pope Leo XIII) ***PROVIDENTISSIMUS DEUS*** (November 18th 1893) Article # 20; ***Denzinger*** (The Sources of Catholic Dogma), Translated by Roy J. Deferrari, from the Thirtieth (30th) Edition, Published by B. Herder Book Co., St. Louis, Mo., and London, W.C., 1957, p. 245, Article # 784; Cf. ***Decrees of the Ecumenical Councils***, Volume Two: Trent to Vatican II, Edited by Norman P. Tanner, S.J., Published by Sheed & Ward, Georgetown University, 1990, p. 664; See also: ***The Christian Faith*** edited by Jacques Dupius, Seventh Revised and Enlarged Edition, Published by Alba House, New York, 2001, Article # 213, p. 103; Lastly see: ***Enchiridion smybolorum*** by Henrici Denzinger, Editio XLIII (43), Collaborated and Translated by Peter Hunermann and Robert Fastiggi (43rd edition), Published by Ignatius Press, San Francisco, (German ed. 2010; English Edition 2012), Article # 1504, p. 371.

His Holiness of Blessed Memory Pope Leo XIII (1893 A.D.) declares and defines the following:

"The Professor, following the tradition of antiquity, will make use of the Vulgate as his text; for the Council of Trent decreed that 'in public lectures, disputations, preaching, and exposition,'(*Sess.* iv., *decr. de edit. et usu sacr. libror.*) the Vulgate is the 'authentic' version; and this is the existing custom of the Church. At the same time, the other versions which Christian antiquity has approved, should not be neglected, more especially the more ancient MSS. For although the meaning of the Hebrew and Greek is substantially rendered by the Vulgate, nevertheless wherever there may be ambiguity or want of clearness, the 'examination of older tongues,' (*De doctr. chr.* iii., 4.) to quote St. Augustine, will be useful and advantageous. But in this matter we need hardly say that the greatest prudence is required, for the 'office of a commentator,' as St. Jerome says, 'is to set forth not what he himself would prefer, but what his author says.' (*Ad Pammachium.*) The question of 'readings' having been, when necessary, carefully discussed, the next thing is to investigate and expound the meaning."[196]

---

[196] The Papal Encyclical ***PROVIDENTISSIMUS DEUS*** 18th of November 1893, Article # 13.

His Holiness of Blessed Memory Pope Pius XII (1943 A.D.) reiterates the following:

"Hence this special authority or as they say, authenticity of the Vulgate was not affirmed by the Council (of Trent) particularly for critical reasons, but rather because of its legitimate use in the Churches throughout so many centuries; by which use indeed the same is shown, in the sense in which the Church has understood and understands it, to be free from any error whatsoever in matters of faith and morals; so that, as the Church herself testifies and affirms, it may be quoted safely and without fear of error in disputations, in lectures and in preaching; and so its authenticity is not specified primarily as critical, but rather as juridical."[197]

Here is the major problem—*the "Original"*[198] *texts of Holy Writ (Scripture) do not exist in their "original(s)"*[199].

---

[197] The Papal Encyclical ***DIVINO AFFLANTE SPIRITU*** September 30th 1943, Article # 21.

[198] Those men that were responsible for writing down their "original(s)" text(s).

[199] Copies of copies are not Original(s).

To make mockery of this (Sacred Passage of Scripture: 1 John 5:7) the pseudo-Authors one a layman the other a so-called priest of the Vatican II (1962-1965) Sect of Perdition raise these idea(s):

1.) "The decree of the Holy Office of 13th January 1897 regarding the authenticity of the *Comma johanneum* (*ASS* 29 [1896-97], 637), which wanted to authoritively explain a question of text criticism, is a typical example of the attitude in the Roman circles."[200]

The second statement is by the pseudo-Priest (Béchard) Dean P., Pseudo-S.J., supposedly of the Jesuits, of whom Avery Dulles, S.J. Pseudo-Cardinal and Pseudo-Jesuit endorses Béchard book, makes this argument in his more than "heretical book" (pathetic work of garbage) with the following pseudo-words:

2.) "The Holy Office, likewise, permitted, and still does permit, Catholic exegetes to study the question of the *Comma Joanneum*, and 'after having well considered the arguments for both sides, with the moderation and circumspection which the gravity of the matter require, even to favor the opinion which stands against the genuineness of the text.'[201] The author of the pamphlet in question forgets or conceals all these facts in order to discredit the work of Catholic commentators, who,

---

[200] Footnote # 7 in original writing(s) of Hubert Jedin, ***The Church in the Industrial Age***; Edited by Hubert Jedin and John Dolan, Published by [1980] 1981 Crossroad Publishing Company, Volume IX, p. 433.

[201] Footnote in original writing(s): Sacred Congregation of the Holy Office, Declaration Concerning the Decree on the Authentic Text of I John 5:7, June 2, 1927 [*EB* 135- 36].

> faithful to Catholic traditions and to the norms taught by the supreme authority of the Church, prove by the very fact of their exacting and difficult labors in textual criticism in what great veneration they hold the Sacred Text."[202]

Furthermore, here is the problem with these pseudo-Text(s) supposedly endorsed by the Pope(s) of Rome? 1. The Holy Office (whether they knew it or not) are not infallible witnesses to Holy Scripture; 2ndly, did they animate from these so-called "true" sources?

His Holiness of Blessed Memory Pope Leo XIII (1893 A.D.) justly, correctly, and infallibly decrees this on the Sacred text of the Vulgate-Bible:

"For all the books which the Church receives as sacred and canonical, are written wholly and entirely, *with all their parts* [emphasis added], at the dictation of the Holy Ghost; and so far is it from being possible that any error can co-exist with inspiration, that inspiration not only is essentially incompatible with error, but excludes and rejects it as absolutely and necessarily as it is impossible that God Himself, the supreme Truth, can utter that which is not true."[203]

---

[202] ***The Scripture Documents*** *An Anthology of Official Catholic Teaching* by Edited and Translated by Dean P. Béchard, S.J., Published by Liturgical Press, Collegeville, Minnesota, 2001, p. 217.

[203] The Papal Encyclical ***PROVIDENTISSIMUS DEUS*** November 18th 1893, Article # 20.

His Holiness of Blessed Memory Pope Pius XII (1943 A.D.) correctly-observed that:

"The sacred Council of Trent ordained by solemn decree that 'the entire books *with all their parts* [emphasis added by author], as they have been wont to be read in the Catholic Church and are contained in the old vulgate Latin edition, are to be held sacred and canonical (Session IV, decr. 1; *Ench. Bibl.* n. 45.).' "[204]

Therefore, it is pristine (that only) The Pope(s) of Rome are Infallible and their legitimate-successors even to the point that the "Roman Catechism" or "so-called" "Catechism of Trent" has in it:

"Official documents have occasionally been issued by Popes to explain certain points of Catholic teaching to individuals, or to local Christian communities; whereas *the Roman Catechism* comprises practically the whole body of Christian doctrine, and is addressed to the whole Church. Its teaching is not infallible; but it holds a place between approved catechisms and what is *de fide* (Footnote: *A Compendium of Catech. Instruction, 1. pp. li. lii.*)."[205]

---

[204] The Papal Encyclical ***DIVINO AFFLANTE SPIRITU*** September 30th 1943, Article # 1.

[205] ***Catechism of the Council of Trent*** Translated into English with Notes by John A. Mchugh, O.P., and, Charles J. Callan, O.P., Published by Preserving Christian Publications, Boonville, New York, [original 1923] cited version: 2021, p. xxxvi.

Only, therefore, is the Roman Pontiff infallible on Faith and Morals and him and him alone—the counterfeit sect (that has destroyed billions of hearts and souls into the fires of hell) is the Vatican II (1962-1965) Sect of Perdition. Likewise, a "no signed" document from the Roman Pontiff is universally-worthless without his immediate and supreme-authority.

His Holiness of Blessed Memory Saint Pope Julius I (6th February 337 to 12th April 352 † A.D.) testifies and instructs the following:

"(2) They say that the Son, our Lord Jesus Christ, is not the proper and true Logos of the almighty God, but a Logos distinct from God, and a distinct Wisdom and Power, that, made by God, he was merely called 'Logos' and 'Wisdom' and 'Power;' and, since this is their view, they say that he is a second hypostasis, separate from the Father [footnote # 4 on page: 19]. Furthermore, they declare in their writings that the Father existed before the Son [*Ast. Soph., frag. 14*; see p. 18], and that he is not truly a Son from God. And, even when they say, he is 'from God;' they mean just as all things are from God. Furthermore, they even dare to say, 'There was once a time when he did not exist' [footnote in the Greek text: *Symb. nic.* (325); see p. 18]; and that he is a 'creature' and a 'created being' [footnote ; *Ast. Soph., frag.* 63; on p. 18]; and, thus, separate him from the Father (see footnote # 5 p. 19). I am convinced that those who say such things are no true citizens of the Catholic Church."[206]

---

[206] ***The LIBRARY OF EARLY CHRISTIANITY*** (VOLUME 3) The Correspondence Pope Julius I (Letter I), Translated (Greek, Latin, into English) by

"They have testified to Athanasius' way of life and have declared that, throughout, he has been the victim of a conspiracy. Again, although it was previously claimed that Athanasius did away with a certain bishop Arsenius, we have discovered that he is, in fact, alive and remains in friendship with him (cf. footnote # 27 of page number: 59)!"[207]

Therefore, the Latin Vulgate Bible (1592 A.D.) stands erect amidst the pollution and heresies of this world. Nota Bene (Good note): he that denies the Council of Trent (December 13th, 1545 to December 4th , 1563 A.D.) is going to be damned if he dies without true penance for his sins and the true Catholic faith founded only in the Sacramental waters of Baptism and the Holy Ghost (John 3:5). To interpret, or add any commentary whatsoever is, strongly prohibited by the

---

Glen L. Thompson, Published by The Catholic University of America, Washington D.C., 2015, p. 19.

[207] ***The LIBRARY OF EARLY CHRISTIANITY*** (VOLUME 3) The Correspondence Pope Julius I (Letter II), Translated (Greek, Latin, into English) by Glen L. Thompson, Published by The Catholic University of America, Washington D.C., 2015, pp. 57-59: footnote # 27 reads: *By early 334 some Melitians had forwarded to the Eusebians a charge that Athanasius had arranged the murder of Arsenius, bishop of Hypsele. Arsenius, however, was found alive and well in Tyre* (Ath., Apol. sec. 8, 65; Soz., H. e. 2.25.10). *Julius uses the case of Arsenius as an example of a charge leveled against Athanasius that was later found to be baseless.*

Council of Trent (16th)[208] with the curse of Almighty God and He Alone! Furthermore, only the Latin Vulgate Bible is "infallible" no other (translation) is "infallible" save the Latin Vulgate Bible (1592 A.D.) by Complete and Full Power of His Holiness of Blessed Memory Pope Clement VIII (24th February 1536 – 3rd March 1605 † A.D.). The abominable Jews are behind the so-called lies of Jesus Christ (The Blessed Trinity): Father, Son, and Holy Ghost—Three Divine Persons—yet One True Eternal God[209].

"Ut unum Deum in Trinitate, et Trinitatem in unitate veneremur—(Translation mine): that We worship one God in Trinity, and Trinity in unity."[210]

The Latin Vulgate Bible (1592 A.D.) has in it (1 John 5:7):

---

[208] To tamper, interpret, subtract or add to the Canons and Decrees of the Holy Ecumenical 19th Council of the Church (**TRENT**) is evil, scandalous, and heretical. Dear reader, please, in love I write this, the Council of Trent in the person of **Pope Pius IV** ***bulla*** (*bull*) ***Benedictus Deus*** (January 26th 1564) explicitly states: —Furthermore, in order to avoid the distortion and confusion that could arise if it were permitted to every individual, as he pleased, to publish his own interpretations and commentaries on the decrees of the council: by apostolic authority We order to all ... that none, without Our authorization, should dare to publish any commentaries, glosses, notes, explanations, or any kind of interpretation at all concerning the decrees of the said council or to stipulate anything, by any authority whatsoever, even on the pretext of greater confirmation or execution of the decrees, or for any other exalted reason‖ (***Enchiridion smybolorum by Henrici Denzinger***, Editio XLIII (43), Collaborated and Translated by *Peter Hunermann and Robert Fastiggi* (43rd edition), Published by Ignatius Press, San Francisco, (German ed. 2010; English Edition 2012), Article # 1849, p. 432).

[209] 1 John 5:7.

[210] ***The Athanasian Creed*** from the 4th century by **Saint Athanasius**.

18. Timor non est in caritate; sed perfecta caritas foras mittit timorem, quoniam timor pœnam habet; qui autem timet, non est perfectus in caritate.

19. Nos ergo diligamus Deum, quoniam Deus prior dilexit nos.

20. Si quis dixerit: quoniam diligo Deum; et fratrem suum oderit, mendax est. Qui enim non diligit fratrem suum, quem videt: Deum, quem non videt, quomodo potest diligere?

21. Et hoc mandatum habemus a Deo, ut, qui diligit Deum, diligat et fratrem suum. (*Supr.* 3, 11. *Eph.* 5, 2.)

CAPUT V.

1. Omnis, qui credit, quoniam Jesus est Christus, ex Deo natus est. Et omnis, qui diligit eum, qui genuit, diligit et eum, qui natus est ex eo.

2. In hoc cognoscimus, quoniam diligimus natos Dei, cum Deum diligamus, et mandata ejus faciamus.

3. Hæc est enim caritas Dei, ut mandata ejus custodiamus; et mandata ejus gravia non sunt.

4. Quoniam omne, quod natum est ex Deo, vincit mundum, et hæc est victoria, quæ vincit mundum, fides nostra.

5. Quis est, qui vincit mundum? nisi qui credit, quoniam Jesus est Filius Dei? (I. *Cor.* 15, 57.)

6. Hic est, qui venit per aquam et sanguinem, Jesus Christus, non in aqua solum, sed in aqua et sanguine. Et Spiritus est, qui testificatur, quoniam Christus est veritas.

7. Quoniam tres sunt, qui testimonium dant in cœlo: Pater, Verbum, et Spiritus sanctus; et hi tres unum sunt.

8. Et tres sunt, qui testimonium dant in terra: Spiritus, et aqua, et sanguis; et hi tres unum sunt.

9. Si testimonium hominum accipimus, testimonium Dei majus est, quoniam hoc est testimonium Dei, quod majus est, quoniam testificatus est de Filio suo.

10. Qui credit in Filium Dei, habet testimonium Dei in se. Qui non credit Filio, mendacem facit eum, quia non credit in testimonium, quod testificatus est Deus de Filio suo. *

11. Et hoc est testimonium, quoniam vitam æternam dedit nobis Deus. Et hæc vita in Filio ejus est.

12. Qui habet Filium, habet vitam; qui non habet Filium, vitam non habet. *(*Joan.* 3, 36.)

13. Hæc scribo vobis, ut sciatis, quoniam vitam habetis æternam, qui creditis in nomine Filii Dei.

14. Et hæc est fiducia, quam habemus ad eum: Quia, quodcumque petierimus secundum voluntatem ejus, audit nos.

15. Et scimus, quia audit nos, quidquid petierimus: scimus, quoniam habemus petitiones, quas postulamus ab eo.

16. Qui scit, fratrem suum peccare peccatum non ad mortem, petat, et dabitur ei vita, peccanti non ad mortem. Est peccatum ad mortem, non pro illo dico, ut roget quis.

17. Omnis iniquitas peccatum est; et est peccatum ad mortem.

18. Scimus, quia omnis, qui natus est ex Deo, non peccat: sed generatio Dei conservat eum, et malignus non tangit eum.

19. Scimus, quoniam ex Deo sumus, et mundus totus in maligno positus est.

20. Et scimus, quoniam Filius Dei venit, et dedit nobis sensum, ut cognoscamus verum Deum, et simus in vero Filio ejus. Hic est verus Deus, et vita æterna. (*Luc.* 24, 45.)

21. Filioli, custodite vos a simulacris. Amen.

CAP. V.

De vera caritate, et de tribus, quae Christo testimonium exhibent. De peccato ad mortem.

1. Omnis, qui credit, quoniam Jesus est Christus, ex Deo natus est[v]. Et omnis, qui diligit eum, qui genuit, diligit et eum, qui natus est ex eo.

2. In hoc[w] cognoscimus, quoniam diligimus natos Dei, cum Deum diligamus, et mandata ejus faciamus.

3. Haec est enim charitas Dei, ut mandata ejus custodiamus; et mandata ejus gravia non sunt[x].

4. Quoniam omne, quod natum est ex Deo, vincit[y] mundum; et haec est victoria, quae vincit mundum, fides nostra.

5. Quis est, qui vincit mundum, nisi qui credit[z], quoniam Jesus est Filius Dei?

6. Hic est, qui venit per aquam et sanguinem, Jesus Christus, non in aqua solum, sed in aqua et sanguine. Et spiritus est, qui testificatur, quoniam Christus est veritas.

7. Quoniam tres sunt, qui testimonium dant in coelo: Pater, Verbum, et Spiritus sanctus; et hi tres unum sunt.

8. Et tres sunt, qui testimonium dant in terra: Spiritus, et aqua, et sanguis; et hi tres unum sunt.

9. Si testimonium hominum accipimus, testimonium Dei majus est. Quoniam hoc est testimonium Dei, quod majus est, quoniam testificatus est de Filio suo.

10. Qui credit in Filium Dei, habet testimonium Dei in se; qui non credit Filio, mendacem facit eum; quia non credit in testimonium, quod testificatus est Deus de Filio suo.

11. Et hoc est testimonium, quoniam vitam aeternam dedit nobis Deus; et haec vita[a] in Filio ejus est.

12. Qui habet Filium, habet vitam[b]; qui non habet Filium, vitam non habet.

13. Haec scribo vobis, ut sciatis, quoniam vitam habetis aeternam, qui creditis in nomine Filii Dei.

14. Et haec est fiducia[c], quam habemus ad eum: quia quodcumque petierimus, secundum voluntatem ejus, audit nos.

15. Et scimus, quia audit nos quidquid petierimus; scimus quoniam habemus petitiones, quas postulamus ab eo.

16. Qui scit fratrem suum peccare peccatum non ad mortem[d], petat, et dabitur ei vita peccanti non ad mortem. Est peccatum

[v] Joh. 1, 12. 13. [w] c. 3, 19. [x] Matth. 11, 30. [y] Joh. 16, 33. [z] c. 4, 15.

[a] Joh. 1, 4. [b] Joh. 3, 36. [c] c. 3, 21. [d] Matth. 12, 32.

CAP. V.

De vera caritate, et de tribus, quae Christo testimonium exhibent. De peccato ad mortem.

1. Omnis, qui credit, quoniam Jesus est Christus, ex Deo natus est[v]. Et omnis, qui diligit eum, qui genuit, diligit et eum, qui natus est ex eo.

2. In hoc[w] cognoscimus, quoniam diligimus natos Dei, cum Deum diligamus, et mandata ejus faciamus.

3. Haec est enim charitas Dei, ut mandata ejus custodiamus; et mandata ejus gravia non sunt[x].

4. Quoniam omne, quod natum est ex Deo, vincit[y] mundum; et haec est victoria, quae vincit mundum, fides nostra.

5. Quis est, qui vincit mundum, nisi qui credit[z], quoniam Jesus est Filius Dei?

6. Hic est, qui venit per aquam et sanguinem, Jesus Christus, non in aqua solum, sed in aqua et sanguine. Et spiritus est, qui testificatur, quoniam Christus est veritas.

7. Quoniam tres sunt, qui testimonium dant in coelo: Pater, Verbum, et Spiritus sanctus; et hi tres unum sunt.

8. Et tres sunt, qui testimonium dant in terra: Spiritus, et aqua, et sanguis; et hi tres unum sunt.

9. Si testimonium hominum accipimus, testimonium Dei majus est. Quoniam hoc est testimonium Dei, quod majus est, quoniam testificatus est de Filio suo.

10. Qui credit in Filium Dei, habet testimonium Dei in se; qui non credit Filio, mendacem facit eum; quia non credit in testimonium, quod testificatus est Deus de Filio suo.

11. Et hoc est testimonium, quoniam vitam aeternam dedit nobis Deus; et haec vita[a] in Filio ejus est.

12. Qui habet Filium, habet vitam[b]; qui non habet Filium, vitam non habet.

13. Haec scribo vobis, ut sciatis, quoniam vitam habetis aeternam, qui creditis in nomine Filii Dei.

14. Et haec est fiducia[c], quam habemus ad eum: quia quodcumque petierimus, secundum voluntatem ejus, audit nos.

15. Et scimus, quia audit nos quidquid petierimus; scimus quoniam habemus petitiones, quas postulamus ab eo.

16. Qui scit fratrem suum peccare peccatum non ad mortem[d], petat, et dabitur ei vita peccanti non ad mortem. Est peccatum

[v] Joh. 1, 12. 13. [w] c. 3, 19. [x] Matth. 11, 30. [y] Joh. 16, 33. [z] c. 4, 15.

[a] Joh. 1, 4. [b] Joh. 3, 36. [c] c. 3, 21. [d] Matth. 12, 32.

Cap. V. 1. diligit eum (*omiss.* et, *altero loco*). 6. 7. et 8. *ita legitur:* hic est, qui venit per aquam et sanguinem, Jesus Christus, non in aqua solum, sed in aqua et sanguine, et spiritus est qui testificatur, quoniam Christus est veritas. Quia tres sunt, qui testimonium dant spiritus et aqua et sanguis, et tres unum sunt (*V. Fascimile in calce hujus editionis*). 9. quia (*bis*). 10. in filio Dei; *ibid.* non credit (*omiss.* filio); *ibid.* quoniam non credidit; *ibid.* in testimonio. 11. in filio ejus (*omiss.* est). 12. filium Dei (*altero loco*). 13. scripsi. 15. scimus quoniam (*primo loco*). 16. petit et dabit ei; *ibid.* vitam peccantibus.

10. In hoc est charitas, non quasi nos dilexerimus Deum, sed quoniam ipse prior dilexit nos, et misit Filium suum propitiationem pro peccatis nostris.

11. Charissimi! si sic Deus dilexit nos, et nos debemus alterutrum diligere.

12. Deum nemo vidit unquam*; si diligamus invicem, Deus in nobis manet, et charitas ejus in nobis perfecta est. *Joh. 1, 18.

13. In hoc cognoscimus, quoniam in eo manemus, et ipse in nobis, quoniam de Spiritu a) suo dedit nobis*. *c. 3, 24. Joh. 14, 17.

14. Et nos vidimus, et testificamur*, quoniam Pater misit filium suum Salvatorem mundi. *Joh. 1, 14.

15. Quisquis confessus fuerit, quoniam Jesus est Filius Dei, Deus in eo manet, et ipse in Deo.

16. Et nos cognovimus, et credidimus charitati, quam habet Deus in nobis. Deus charitas est*; et qui manet in charitate, in Deo manet, et Deus in eo. *v. 8.

17. In hoc perfecta est charitas Dei nobiscum, ut fiduciam habeamus in die judicii*; quia sicut ille est, et nos sumus in hoc mundo. *c. 2, 28.

18. Timor non est in charitate; sed perfecta charitas foras mittit timorem. Quoniam timor poenam habet; qui autem timet, non est perfectus in charitate.

19. Nos ergo diligamus Deum, quoniam Deus prior dilexit nos*. *v. 10.

20. Si quis dixerit, quoniam diligo Deum, et fratrem suum oderit, mendax* est; qui enim non diligit fratrem suum, quem videt, Deum, quem non videt, quomodo potest diligere? *c. 2, 4. 11.

21. Et hoc mandatum* habemus a Deo: ut qui diligit Deum, diligat et fratrem suum. *Marc. 12, 31.

a) 1590. add. sancto

Cap. 5.

De vera charitate, et de tribus Christo testimonium reddentibus. De peccato ad mortem.

1. Omnis, qui credit, quoniam Jesus est Christus, ex Deo natus est*. Et omnis, qui diligit eum, qui genuit, diligit et eum, qui natus est ex eo. *Joh. 1, 12. 13.

2. In hoc* cognoscimus, quoniam diligimus natos Dei, cum Deum diligamus, et mandata ejus faciamus. *c. 3, 19.

3. Haec est enim charitas Dei, ut mandata ejus custodiamus; et mandata ejus gravia non sunt*. *Matth. 11, 30.

4. Quoniam omne, quod natum est ex Deo, vincit* mundum; et haec est victoria, quae vincit mundum, fides nostra. *Joh. 16, 33.

5. Quis est, qui vincit mundum, nisi qui credit*, quoniam Jesus est Filius Dei? *c. 4, 15.

6. Hic est, qui venit per aquam et sanguinem, Jesus Christus, non in aqua solum, sed in aqua et sanguine. Et spiritus est, qui testificatur, quoniam Christus est veritas.

7. Quoniam tres sunt, qui testimonium dant in coelo: Pater, Verbum, et Spiritus sanctus; et hi tres unum sunt.

8. Et tres sunt, qui testimonium dant in terra: Spiritus, et aqua, et sanguis; et hi tres unum sunt.

9. Si testimonium hominum accipimus, testimonium Dei majus est. Quoniam hoc est testimonium Dei, quod majus est, quoniam testificatus est de Filio suo.

10. Qui credit in Filium Dei, habet testimonium Dei in se; qui non credit Filio, mendacem facit eum; quia non credit in testimonium, quod testificatus est Deus de Filio suo.

11. Et hoc est testimonium,

All of these texts are legitmate to ***Johnnaine Comma***[211]; it is a Part of Holy Scripture and rightly so! The dirty-rotten Jews have done nothing more than a smear-campign against Christ (God). They have lied and caused the greatest of confusion(s) in the time of Christ (God) and to the present day! Remember, that Christ (God) will be virtorious and put down all His-enemies in the end. Don't give up! Don't fall into despair, doubt, denial, or temptation, or suicide, know that Christ (God) will defend thee even in thy darkest moment(s). To die in Mortal sin or Heresy is the greatest of evil that can befallen any of us at anytime. Please, stop and unite thy suffereings with the suffering of Christ (God). Christ (God) is waiting for us to response to His beckon and carry our cross for Him, with Him, and in Him, now, and, at the hour of our deaths. There are three things with which we must be found with (if we die) and want to go to Heaven:

1. The Catholic faith
2. Tears of penance (for our sins) no original/mortal sin(s).
3. The Holy Sacrament of Baptism (John 3:5) to wash away Original or Mortal/Venial sin(s).

My friend please I beg of thee take my warning serious! Thank you for reading this short work of mine. Furthermore, if we do not take Christ (God) at His word will we take the Pope (Bishop of Rome) at his word(s)? When the Pope says something take it as he means/writes (says) it! Amen.

---

[211] 1 John 5:7.

Index

Examination of Conscience

CONFESSING MY SINS:

"*O' God, have mercy upon me a sinner.*" (Luke 18:13).

"*Behold the Lamb of God. Behold him who taketh away the sin of the world.*" (John 1:29).

"*If you love me, keep my commandments.*" (John 14:15).

"*Whose sins you shall remit, they are remitted them: and whose sins you shall retain, they are retained.*" (John 20:23).

The Five Steps of Confession:

(Pray to God the Holy Ghost for His light and grace to see thy sins).

1. Examine thy conscience.
2. Be sorry for thy sins; try to have the perfect sorrow of love.
3. Make a firm resolution not to sin again, and to avoid the near occasions of sin.
4. Confess all thy sins to God the Father, God the Son, and God the Holy Ghost—Three Divine Persons (Matthew 28:19)—yet One True Eternal God (1 John 5:7).
5. Do penance for thy sins and amend thy life.

I BELIEVE in Thee, O' God, Father, Son, and Holy Ghost, my Creator, my Redeemer, and my Sanctifier; I believe Thou art all-holy, just and merciful. I believe that Thou art willing to pardon and to save me, if I do penance and forsake my sins. O' my God, strengthen and increase my faith, and grant me the grace of a true penance, for Jesus Christ's sake. Amen.

Tell Christ (God) the specific kind of sins thou hast committed against Him, and do the best of thy ability, how many times thou committed them. If thou art in doubt if thy sin be mortal or venial—still confess it to Christ. Remember that Christ (God) is there to remit thee of thy sins and the punishment due to thy sins, so do not be afraid to confess all thy sins to Him.

1. Have I neglected the knowledge of my faith as taught in the Apostles Creed, the Ten Commandments, and Seven Sacraments, the Our Father etc? Have I deliberately doubted or denied any teachings of the Church? Have I taken part in *any* non-Catholic worship? Have I practiced any superstitions (such as witchcraft, horoscopes, fortune-telling, Ouija board, Satanism etc.)? Have I thought about becoming a Freemason or did I enter a Lodge out of curiosity or am I currently a member of a Secret Society like the Freemasons?

2. Did I curse or swear? Did I use God's (Christ) name in vain: lightly...carelessly...by blasphemy? Do I use profane language? Have I insulted sacred persons such as (the Eucharist, the Blessed Virgin Mary, the Saints)?

3. Did I do unnecessary servile (laborious) work on Sunday? Did I respect God (Christ) and rest (or retire) from work and pray and honor Him that day of Sunday!

4. Did I honor and obey my parents? Others with lawful authority? Have I talked back? Failed to help at home? Been sad or sour? Neglected my children's religious education? failed to lead them to Prayer...or to frequent God's Mercy? failed to spend time with my family? Separated or divorced civilly without consultation according to the mind of the Church and Her Teaching?

5. Was I angry...resentful...kept hatred in my heart? Did I fight...give bad example or scandal? Did I fail to correct in charity? Permitted or encouraged an abortion or mutilation (vasectomy, etc.) to avoid children? Did I murder someone? Did I get a tattoo(s) (mutilate) my body?

6. Did I consent to impure glances? Passionate kisses? Sinful touches? Was I immodest in dress or behavior? Did I read or watch pornography, or impure magazines? Am I guilty of masturbation (impurity with self), fornication (premarital sex), adultery (sex with a married person), homosexuality (same-sex relations), or birth control (by pills, devices, withdrawal, or another means etc.)? Do I avoid laziness, gluttony, idleness, and the occasions of impurity?

7. Did I steal? What or how much? Did I return it or make equal restitution in some way? Did I waste time at work, in school, at home? Am I stingy? Do I gamble excessively? Neglect to pay my debts promptly? Do I live poverty of spirit or detachment? Have I supported the Roman Catholic Faith by prayer and works of charity?

8. Have I gossiped? Talked about another behind his back? Do I always tell the truth? Am I sincere? Did I reveal secrets that should have been kept confidential? Am I negative or uncharitable in my talk? Have I told lies?

9. Have I consented to impure thoughts? Have I caused them by stares, bad reading, curiosity or impure conversations? Do I neglect to control my imagination? Do I pray at once to banish such bad thoughts and temptations?

10. Is my heart greedy? Am I jealous of what another has? Am I envious of him because I don't have what he has? Am I moody? Gloomy? Do I work, study and keep busy to counter idle thoughts? Is my heart set on earthly possessions or on the true treasures in Heaven?

ACT OF CONTRITION:

"O my God, I am heartily sorry for having offended Thee and I detest all my sins, because I dread the loss of heaven and the pains of hell, but most of all because they offend Thee, my God, who are all good and deserving of all my love. I firmly resolve, with the help of Thy grace, to confess my sins, to do penance and to amend my life. Amen."

Have confidence in Christ's mercy!

"Let all poor sinners, as well as Jews, Muslims, and Heretics come to My Divine Mercy and rest is assured that if they come with a contrite heart and a resolve not to sin any more I will pardon all their sins. There is no sin, which I cannot pardon. And I thirst for thy heart to be one with Me if only thou wilt take My hand and trust in My Divine Mercy which I give to all those that believe and trust in Me and My Most Holy Catholic Church and receive the Holy Sacrament of Baptism. Do not be afraid to come to Me, and seek refuge and comfort, no matter how great the sin. I died for thee."

Dominie Iesus Christe, Fili Dei, Miserere Mihi Peccatori.

Lord Jesus Christ, Son of God, Have Mercy Upon Me a Sinner.

The Nicene Creed

I BELIEVE in one God, the Father Almighty, Maker of heaven and earth, of all things visible and invisible.

And in one Lord Jesus Christ, the Only Begotten Son of God, born of the Father before all ages. God from God; Light from Light; true God from true God; begotten, not made, being of one substance with the Father, by whom all things were made.

Who for us men, and for our salvation, came down from heaven [Here all kneel down.], and was incarnate by the Holy Ghost of the Virgin Mary:

AND WAS MADE MAN.

He was crucified also for us, suffered under Pontius Pilate, and was buried. The third day He rose again according to the Scriptures; and ascended into Heaven, and sitteth at the right hand of the Father: And He shall come again with glory to judge both the living and the dead: of whose kingdom there shall be no end.

And I believe in the Holy Ghost, the Lord and Giver of Life, who proceedeth from the Father and the Son: Who together with the Father and the Son is worshipped and glorified; who spoke by the Prophets.

And One Holy Catholic and Apostolic Church.

I confess one Baptism for the remission of sins. And I look for the Resurrection of the dead, and the life of the world to come. Amen.

CHRONOLOGICAL LIST OF THE ROMAN PONTIFFS

SAINT PETER
Simon of Bethsaida (Galilee)
died ca. A.D. 64.

St. Linus (Tuscia) ca. 67—76
St. Anacletus (Rome) ca. 76—ca. 91
St. Clement I (Rome) ca. 91—ca. 101
St. Evaristus (Greece) ca. 100—ca. 109
St. Alexander I (Rome) ca. 109—ca. 116
St. Sixtus I (Rome) ca. 116—ca. 125
St. Telesphorus (Greece) ca. 125—ca. 136
St. Hyginus (Greece) ca. 138—ca. 140
St. Pius I (Aquileia) ca. 140—ca. 155
St. Anicetus (Syria) ca. 155—ca. 166
St. Soter (Campania) ca. 166—ca. 174
St. Eleutherius, or Eleutherus (Nicopolis) ca. 174—ca. 189
St. Victor I (Africa) 189—198
St. Zephyrinus (Rome) 198—217
St. Callistus I [often Calixtus] (Rome) 217—222
St. Urban I (Rome) 222—230
St. Pontian (Rome) 21 July 230—28 Sept. 235
St. Anterus (Greece) 21 Nov. 233—3 Jan. 236
St. Fabian (Rome) 10 Jan. 236—20 Jan. 250
St. Cornelius (Rome) Mar. 251—June 253
St. Lucius I (Rome) 25 June 253—5 Mar. 254
St. Stephen I (Rome) 12 May 254—2 Aug. 257
St. Sixtus II (Greece) Aug. 257—6 Aug. 258
St. Dionysius [birthplace unknown] 22 July 259—26 Dec. 268

St. Felix I (Rome) 3 Jan. 269—30 Dec. 274

St. Eutychian (Luni) 4 Jan. 275—7 Dec. 283

St. Gaius, or Caius (Dalmatia) 17 Dec. 283—22 Apr. 296

St. Marcellinus (Rome) 30 June 296—304; d. 25 Oct. 304

St. Marcellus I (Rome) Nov./Dec. 306—16 Jan. 308

St. Eusebius (Greece) 18 Apr.—21 Oct. 310

St. Miltiades, or Meichiades (Africa) 2 July 311—10 Jan. 314

St. Silvester I (Rome) 31 Jan. 314—31 Dec. 335

St. Mark (Rome) l8 Jan.—7 Oct. 336

St. Julius I (Rome) 6 Feb. 337—12 Apr. 352

Liberius (Rome) 17 May 352—24 Sept. 366

St. Damasus I (Spain) 1 Oct. 366—11 Dec. 384

St. Siricius (Rome) Dec. 384—26 Nov. 399

St. Anastasius I (Rome) 27 Nov. 399—19 Dec. 401

St. Innocent I (Albano) 21 Dec. 401—12 Mar. 417

St. Zosimus (Greece) 18 Mar. 417—26 Dec. 418

St. Boniface I (Rome) 28 Dec. 418—4 Sept. 422

St. Celestine I (Campania) 10 Sept. 422—27 July 432

St. Sixtus, or Xystus, III (Rome) 31 July 432—19 Aug. 440

St. Leo I, "the Great" (Tuscany) Aug./Sept. 440—10 Nov. 461

St. Hilarus, or Hilary of Sardinia 19 Nov. 461—29 Feb. 468

St. Simplicius (Tivoli) 3 Mar. 468—10 Mar. 483

St. Felix III (II) (Rome) 13 Mar. 483—1 Mar. 492

St. Gelasius I (Africa) I Mar. 492—21 Nov. 496

Anastasius II (Rome) 24 Nov. 496—19 Nov. 498

St. Symmachus (Sardinia) 22 Nov. 498—19 July 514

St. Hormisdas (Frosinore) 20 July 514—6 Aug. 523

St. John I (Tuscany) 13 Aug. 523—18 May 526

St. Felix IV (III) (Samnium) 12 July 526—22 Sept. 530

Boniface II (Rome) 22 Sept. 530—17 Oct. 532

John II (Rome) 2 Jan. 533—8 May 535

St. Agapitus I (Rome) 13 May 535—22 April 536

St. Silverius (Campania) 8 June 536—11 Nov. 537; d. 2 Dec. 537

Vigilius (Rome) 29 Mar. 537—7 June 555

Pelagius I (Rome) 16 Apr. 556—3 Mar. 561

John III (Rome) l7 July 561—l3 July 574

Benedict I (Rome) 2 June 575—30 July 579
Pelagius II (Rome) 26 Nov. 579—7 Feb. 590
St. Gregory I, "the Great" (Rome) 3 Sept. 590—12 Mar. 604
Sabinian (Tuscany) 13 Sept. 604—22 Feb. 606
Boniface III (Rome) 19 Feb. —12 Nov. 607
St. Boniface IV (Abruzzi) 15 Sept. 608—8 May 615
St. Deusdedit [later Adeodatus I] (Rome) 19 Oct. 615—8 Nov. 618
Boniface V (Naples) 23 Dec. 619—25 Oct. 625
Honorius I (Campania) 27 Oct. 625—12 Oct. 638
Severinus (Rome) 28 May—2 Aug. 640
John IV (Dalmatia) 24 Dec. 640—12 Oct. 642
Theodore I (Greece) 24 Nov. 642—14 May 649
St. Martin I (Todi) 5 July 649—17 June 653; d. 16 Sept. 655
St. Eugene I (Rome) 10 Aug. 654—2 June 657
St. Vitalian (Segni) 31) July 657—27 Jan. 672
Adeodatus II (Rome) 11 Apr. 672—17 June 676
Donus (Rome) 2 Nov. 676—11 April 678
St. Agatho (Sicily) 27 June 678—10 Jan. 681
St. Leo II (Sicily) 17 Aug. 682—3 July 683
St. Benedict II (Rome) 26 June 684—5 May 685
John V (Syria) 23 July 685—2 Aug. 686
Conon [birthplace unknown] 21 Oct. 686—21 Sept. 687
St. Sergius (Syria) 15 Dec. 687—9 Sept. 701
John VI (Greece) 30 Oct. 701—11 Jan. 705
John VII (Greece) I Mar. 705—18 Oct. 707
Sisinnius (Syria) 15 Jan.—4 Feb. 708
Constantine (Syria) 25 Mar. 708—9 Apr. 715
St. Gregory II (Rome) 19 May 715—11 Feb. 731
St. Gregory III (Syria) 18 Mar. 731—28 Nov. 741
St. Zacharias (Greece) 3 Dec. 741—15 Mar. 752
Stephen II (III) (Rome) 26 Mar. 752—26 Apr. 757
St. Paul I (Rome) 29 May 757—28 June 767
Stephen III (IV) (Sicily) 7 Aug. 768—24 Jan. 772
Hadrian I (Rome) 1 Feb. 772—25 Dec. 795
St. Leo III (Rome) 26 Dec. 795—12 June 816
Stephen IV (V) (Rome) 22 June 816—24 Jan. 817
St. Paschal I (Rome) 24 Jan. 817—11 Feb. 824
Eugene II (Rome) 5 June 824—27 Aug. 827

Valentine (Rome) Aug.—Sept. 827
Gregory IV (Rome) late 827—25 Jan. 844
Sergius II (Rome) Jan. 844—27 Jan. 847
St. Leo IV (Rome) 10 April 847—17 July 855
Benedict III (Rome) 21) Sept. 855—17 Apr. 858
St. Nicholas I, "the Great" (Rome) 24 Apr. 858—13 Nov. 867
Hadrian II (Rome) 14 Dec. 867—Nov. or Dec. 872
John VIII (Rome) 14 Dec. 872—16 Dec. 882
Marinus I (Gallese) 16 Dec. 882—15 May 884
St. Hadrian III (Rome) 17 May 884—mid-Sept.
Stephen V (VI) (Rome) Sept. 885—14 Sept. 891
Formosus (Porto) 6 Oct. 891—4 Apr. 896
Boniface VI (Rome) Apr. 896
Stephen VI (VII) (Rome) May 896—Aug. 897
Romanus (Gallese) Aug.—Nov. 897; d.?
Theodore II (Rome) Nov. 897
John IX (Tivoli) Jan. 898—Jan. 900
Benedict IV (Rome) May/June 900—Aug. 903
Leo V (Ardea) Aug.—Sept. 903; d. early 904
Sergius III (Rome) 29 Jan. 904—14 Apr. 911
Anastasius III (Rome) ca. June 911—ca. Aug. 913
Landus (Sabina) ca. Aug. 913—ca. Mar. 914
John X (Imola) Mar./Apr. 914—May 928 (deposed); d. 929
Leo VI (Rome) May—Dec. 928
Stephen VII (VIII) (Rome) Dec. 928—Feb. 931
John XI (Rome) Feb. or Mar. 931—Dec. 935 or Jan. 936
Leo VII (Rome) 3 Jan. 936—13 July 939
Stephen VIII (IX) (Rome) 14 July 939—late Oct. 942
Marinus II (Rome) 30 Oct. 942—early May 946
Agapitus II (Rome) 10 May 946—Dec. 955
John XII (Tusculum) 16 Dec. 955—14 May 964
Leo VIII (Rome) 4 Dec. 963—1 Mar. 965
Benedict V (Rome) 22 May—23 June 964 (deposed); d. 4 July 966
John XIII (Rome) 1 Oct. 965—6 Sept. 972
Benedict VI (Rome) 19 Jan. 973—July 974
Benedict VII (Rome) Oct. 974—10 July 983
John XIV (Pavia) Dec. 983—20 Aug. 984
John XV (Rome) mid-Aug. 985—Mar. 996

Gregory V (Saxony) 3 May 996—18 Feb. 999

Sylvester II, Gerberto (Auvergne) 2 Apr. 999—12 May 1003

John XVII, Siccone (Rome) 16 May—6 Nov. 1003

John XVIII, Phasianus (Rome) 25 Dec. 1003—June or July 1009

Sergius IV, Peter (Rome) 31 July 1009—12 May 1012

Benedict VIII, Theophylactus (Tusculum) 17 May 1012—9 Apr. 1024

John XIX (Rome) 19 Apr. 1024—20 Oct. 1032

Benedict IX, Theophylactus (Tusculum) 21 Oct. 1032—16 July 1048

Silvester III, John (Rome) 20 Jan.—10 Mar. 1045; d. 1063

Gregory VI, John Gratian (Rome) 1 May 1045— 20 Dec. 1046; d. late 1047

Clement II, Suitger, Lord of Morsleben and Hornburg (Saxony) 24 Dec. 1046—9 Oct. 1047

Damasus II, Poppo (Bavaria) 17 July—9 Aug. 1048

St. Leo IX, Bruno (Alsace) 12 Feb. 1049—19 Apr. 1054

Victor II, Gebhard (Swabia) 13 Apr. 1055—28 July 1057

Stephen IX (X), Frederick (Lorraine) 2 Aug. 1057—29 Mar. 1058

Nicholas II, Gerard (Burgundy) 6 Dec. 1058— 19 or 26 July 1061

Alexander II, Anselm da Baggio (Milan) 30 Sept. 1061—21 April 1073

St. Gregory VII, Hildebrand (Tuscany) 22 Apr. 1073—25 May 1085

Bl. Victor III, Desiderius (Benevento) 24 May 1086—16 Sept. 1087

Bl. Urban II, Otto di Lagery (France) 12 Mar. 1088—29 July 1099

Paschal II, Raniero (Ravenna) 13 Aug. 1099—21 Jan. 1118

Gelasius II, Giovanni Caetani (Gaeta) 24 Jan. 1118—29 Jan. 1119

Callistus II, Guido of Burgundy (Burgundy) 2 Feb. 1119—14 Dec. 1124

Honorius II, Lamberto (Fiagnano) 21 Dec. 1124—13 Feb. 1130

Innocent II, Gregorio Papareschi (Rome) 15/16 Dec. 1130—24 Sept. 1143

Celestine II, Guido (Citta di Castello) 14 Feb. 1143—8 Mar. 1144

Lucius II, Gerardo Caccianemici (Bologna) 12 Mar. 1144—15 Feb. 1145

Bl. Eugene III, Bernardo di Montemagno (Pisa) 15 Feb. 1145—8 July 1153

Anastasius IV, Corrado (Rome) 8 July 1153—3 Dec. 1154

Hadrian IV, Nicholas Breakspear (England) 4 Dec. 1154—1 Sept. 1159

Alexander III, Rolando Bandinelli (Siena) 7 Sept. 1159—30 Aug. 1181

Lucius III, Ubaldo Allucingoli (Lucia) 1 Sept. 1181—25 Nov. 1185

Urban III, Uberto Crivelli (Milan) 25 Nov. 1185—19/20 Oct. 1187

Gregory VIII, Alberto de Morra (Benevento) 21 Oct.—17 Dec. 1187

Clement III, Paolo Scolari (Rome) 19 Dec. 1187—late Mar. 1191

Celestine III, Giacinto Bobone (Rome) Mar./Apr. 1191—8 Jan. 1198

Innocent III, Lotario di Segni (Anagni) 8 Jan. 1198—l6 July 1216

Honorius III, Cencio Savelli (Rome) 18 July 1216—18 Mar. 1227

Gregory IX, Ugolino di Segni (Anagni) l9 Mar. 1227—22 Aug. 241

Celestine IV, Goifredo Castiglione (Milan) 25 Oct.—10 Nov. 1241

Innocent IV, Sinibaldo Fieschi (Genoa) 25 June 1243—7 Dec. 1254

Alexander IV, Rinaldo di Segni (Anagni) 12 Dec. 1254—25 May 1261

Urban IV, Jacques Pantaléon (Troyes) 29 Aug. 1261—2 Oct. 1264

Clement IV, Guy Foulques (France) 5 Feb. 1265—29 Nov. 1268

Bl. Gregory X, Teobaldo Visconti (Piacenza) 1 Sept. 1271—10 Jan. 1276

Bl. Innocent V, Peter of Tarentaise (Savoy) 21 Jan.—22 June 1276

Hadrian V, Ottobono Fieschi (Genoa) 22 July—18 Aug. 1276

John XXI, Petrus Iuliani (Portugal) 8 Sept. 1276—20 May 1277

Nicholas III, Giovanni Gaetano Orsini (Rome) 25 Nov. 1277—22 Aug. 1280

Martin IV, Simon de Brie (France) 22 Feb. 1281—28 Mar. 1285

Honorius IV, Giacorno Savelli (Rome) 2 Apr. 1285—3 Apr. 1287

Nicholas IV, Girolanio Masci (Ascoli) 22 Feb. 1288—4 Apr. 1292

St. Peter Celestine V, Pietro del Murrone (Isernia) 5 July—13 Dec. 1294; d. 19 May 1296

Boniface VIII, Benedetto Caetano (Anagni) 24 Dec. 1294—11 Oct. 1303

Bl. Benedict XI, Nicholas Boccasini (Treviso) 22 Oct. 1303—7 July 1304

Clement V, Bertrand de Got (France) 5 June 1305—20 Apr. 1314

John XXII, Jacques d'Euse (Cahors) 7 Aug. 1316—4 Dec. 1334

Benedict XII, Jacques Fournier (France) 20 Dec. 1334—25 Apr. 1342

Clement VI, Pierre Roger (France) 7 May 1342—6 Dec. 1352

Innocent VI, Etienne Aubert (France) 18 Dec. 1352—12 Sept. 1362

Bl. Urban V, Guillaume de Grimoard (France) 28 Sept. 1362—19 Dec. 1370

Gregory XI, Pierre Roger de Beaufort (France) 30 Dec. 1370—27 Mar. 1378

Urban VI, Bartolomeo Prignano (Naples) 8 Apr. 1378—15 Oct. 1389

Boniface IX, Pietro Tornacelli (Naples) 2 Nov. 1389—1 Oct. 1404

Innocent VII, Cosmo Migliorati (Sulmoua) 17 Oct. 1404—6 Nov. 1406

Gregory XII, Angclo Correr (Venice) 30 Nov. 1406— 4 July 1415; d. 18 Oct. 1417

Martin V, Oddone Colonna (Rome) 11 Nov. 1417—20 Feb. 1431

Eugene IV, Gabriele Condulmer (Venice) 3 Mar. 1431—23 Feb. 1447

Nicholas V, Tommaso Parentucelli (Sarzana) 6 Mar. 1447—24 Mar. 1455

Callistus III, Alfonso Borgia (Jativa, Valencia) 8 Apr. 1455—6 Aug. 1458

Pius II, Enea Silvio Piccolomini (Siena) 19 Aug. 1458—15 Aug. 1464

Paul II, Pietro Barbo (Venice) 30 Aug. 1464—26 July 1471

Sixtus IV, Francesco della Rovere (Savona) 9 Aug. 1471—12 Aug. 1484

Innocent VIII, Giovanni Battista Cibo (Genoa) 29 Aug. 1484—25 July 1492

Alexander VI, Rodrigo de Borgia (Jativa, Valencia) 11 Aug. 1492—18 Aug. 1503

Pius III, Francesco Todeschini—Piccolomini (Siena) 22 Sept.—18 Oct. 1503

Julius II, Guiiano della Rovere (Savona) 1 Nov. 1503—21 Feb. 1513

Leo X, Giovanni de'Medici (Florence) 11 Mar. 1513—I Dec. 1521

Hadrian VI, Adrian Florensz (Utrecht) 9 Jan. 1522—14 Sept. 1523

Clement VII, Giulio de'Medici (Florence) 19 Nov. 1523—25 Sept. 1534

Paul III, Alessandro Farnese (Rome) 13 Oct. 1534—10 Nov. 1549

Julius III, Giovanni Ciocchi del Monte (Rome) 8 Feb. 1550—23 Mar. 1555

Marcellus II, Marcella Cervini (Montepulciano) 9 Apr.—1 May 1555

Paul IV, Gian Pietro Carafa (Naples) 23 May 1555—18 Aug. 1559

Pius IV, Giovan-Angelo de'Medici (Milan) 25 Dec. 1559—9 Dec. 1565

St. Pius V, Antonio Ghislieri (Bosco) 7 Jan. 1566—1 May 1572

Gregory XIII, Ugo Buonncompagni (Bologna) 14 May 1572—10 Apr. 1585

Sixtus V, Felice Peretti (Grottammare) 24 Apr. 1585—27 Aug. 1590

Urban VII, Giambattista Castagna (Rome) 15—27 Sept. 1590

Gregory XIV, Niccolo Sfondrati (Cremona) 5 Dec. 1590—16 Oct. 1591

Innocent IX, Giovan Antonio Facchinetti (Bologna) 29 Oct.—30 Dec. 1591

Clement VIII, Ippolito Aldobrandini (Florence) 30 Jan. 1592—5 Mar. 1605

Leo XI, Alessandro de'Medici (Florence) 1—27 Apr. 1605

Paul V, Camillo Borghese (Rome) 16 May 1605—28 Jan. 1621

Gregory XV, Alessandro Ludovisi (Bologna) 9 Feb. 1621—8 July 1623

Urban VIII, Maffeo Barberini (Florence) 6 Aug. 1623—29 July 1644

Innocent X, Giovanni Battista Painphili (Rome) 15 Sept. 1644—1 Jan. 1655

Alexander VII, Fabio Chigi (Siena) 7 Apr. 1655—22 May 1667

Clement IX, Giulio Rospigliosi (Pistoia) 20 June 1667—9 Dec. 1669

Clement X, Emilio Altieri (Rome) 29 Apr. 1670—22 July 1676

Bl. Innocent XI, Benedetto Odescaichi (Gorno) 21 Sept. 1676—12 Aug. 1689

Alexander VIII, Pietro Ottoboni (Venice) 6 Oct. 1689—1 Feb. 1691

Innocent XII, Antonio Pignatelli (Spinazzola) 12 July 1691—27 Sept. 1700

Clement XI, Giovanni Francesco Albani (Urbino) 23 Nov. 1700—19 Mar. 1721

Innocent XIII, Michelangelo dei Conti, (Rome) 8 May 1721—7 Mar. 1724

Benedict XIII, Pietro Orsini (Gravina) 29 May 1724—21 Feb. 1730

Clement XII, Lorenzo Corsini (Florence) 12 July 1730—6 Feb. 1740

Benedict XIV, Prospero Lambertini (Bologna) 17 Aug. 1740—3 May 1758

Clement XIII, Carlo Rezzonico (Venice) 6 July 1758—2 Feb. 1769

Clement XIV, Giovanni Ganganelli (Rimini) 19 May 1769—22 Sept. 1774

Pius VI, Gionangelo Braschi (Cesena) 15 Feb. 1775—29 Aug. 1799

Pius VII, Barnaba Chiaramonti (Cesena) 14 Mar. 1800—20 July 1823

Leo XII, Annibale della Genga (Fabriano) 28 Sept. 1823—10 Feb. 1829

Pius VIII, Francesco Castiglioni (Cingoli) 31 Mar. 1829—30 Nov. 1830

Gregory XVI, Bartolomeo Cappellari (Belluno) 2 Feb. 1831—1 June 1846

Pius IX, Giovanni Ferretti (Senigallia) 16 June 1846—7 Feb. 1878

Leo XIII, Gioacchino Pecci (Anagni) 20 Feb. 1878—20 July 1903

St. Pius X, Giuseppe Sarto (Treviso) 4 Aug. 1903—20 Aug. 191

Benedict XV, Giacomo della Chiesa (Genoa) 3 Sept. 1914—22 Jan. 1922

Pius XI, Achille Ratti (Milan) 6 Feb. 1922—10 Feb. 1939

Pius XII, Eugenio Pacelli (Rome) 2 Mar. 1939—9 Oct. 1958

List of Ecumenical Councils of the Roman Catholic Church:

1. Nicea [Nicaea] (I), St. Pope Sylvester I, 325 A.D.
2. Constantinople (I), St. Pope Damascus I, 381 A.D.
3. Ephesus, St. Pope Celestine I, 431 A.D.
4. Chalcedon, St. Pope Leo the Great, 451 A.D.
5. Constantinople (II), Pope Vigilius, 553 A.D.
6. Constantinople (III), Sts. Pope Agatho ; Leo II, 680-1 A.D.
7. Nicea [Nicaea] (II), Pope Hadrian I, 787 A.D.
8. Constantinople (IV), Nicholas I ; Hadrian II , 869-870 A.D.
9. Lateran (I), Pope Callistus II, 1123 A.D.
10. Lateran (II), Pope Innocent II, 1139 A.D.
11. Lateran (III), Pope Alexander III, 1179 A.D.
12. Lateran (IV), Pope Innocent III, 1215 A.D.
13. Lyons (I), Pope Innocent IV, 1245 A.D.
14. Lyons (II), Pope Gregory X, 1274 A.D.
15. Vienne [Vienna], Pope Clement V, 1311-1312 A.D.
16. Constance, Pope Martin V, 1414-1418 A.D.
17. Florence, Pope Eugene IV, 1438-1445 A.D.
18. Lateran (V), Popes Julius II ; Leo X, 1512-1517 A.D.
19. Trent, Popes Paul III ; Pius IV, 1545-1563 A.D.
20. Vatican, Pope Pius IX, 1869-1870 A.D.

List of Doctors of the Church:

29 Doctors:

1. Gregory the Great
2. Ambrose
3. Augustine of Hippo
4. Jerome
5. Thomas Aquinas
6. John Chrysostom
7. Basil the Great
8. Gregory of Nazianzus
9. Athanasius
10. Bonaventure
11. Anselm of Canterbury
12. Isidore of Seville
13. Peter Chrysologus
14. Leo the Great
15. Peter Damian
16. Bernard of Clairvaux
17. Hiliary of Poitiers
18. Alphonsus Liguori
19. Francis de Sales

20. Cyril of Alexandria
21. Cyril of Jerusalem
22. John Damascene
23. Bede the Venerable
24. Ephrem
25. Peter Canisius
26. John of the Cross
27. Robert Bellarmine
28. Albertus Magnus
29. Anthony of Padua

www.ingramcontent.com/pod-product-compliance
Ingram Content Group UK Ltd.
Pitfield, Milton Keynes, MK11 3LW, UK
UKHW020140250726
13967UKWH00002B/764